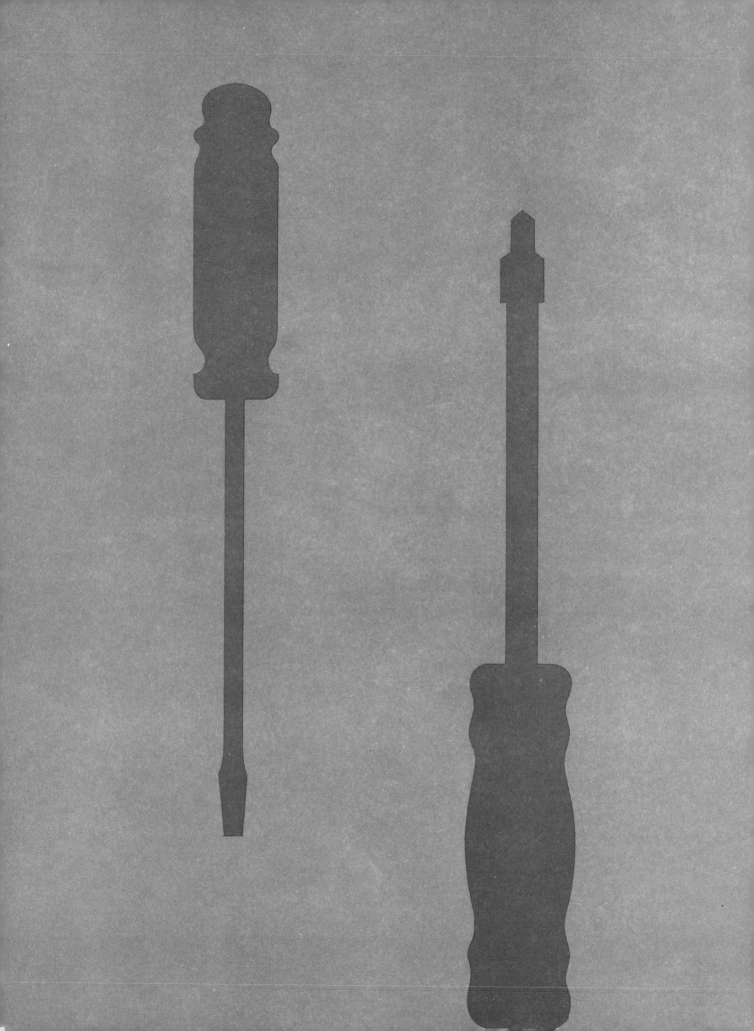

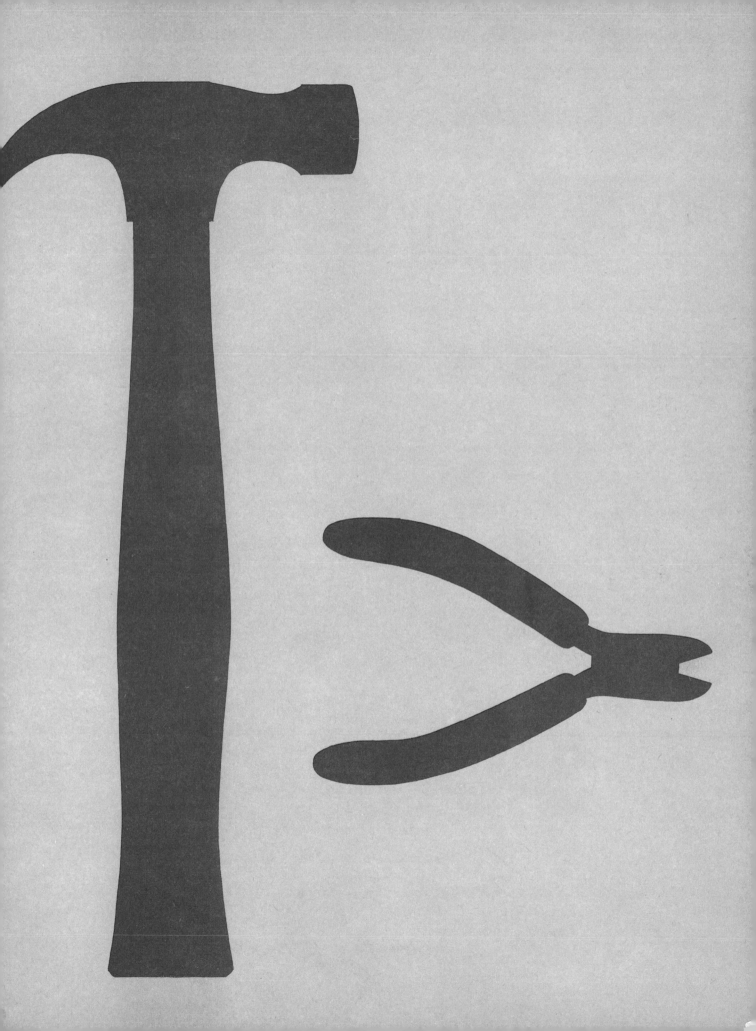

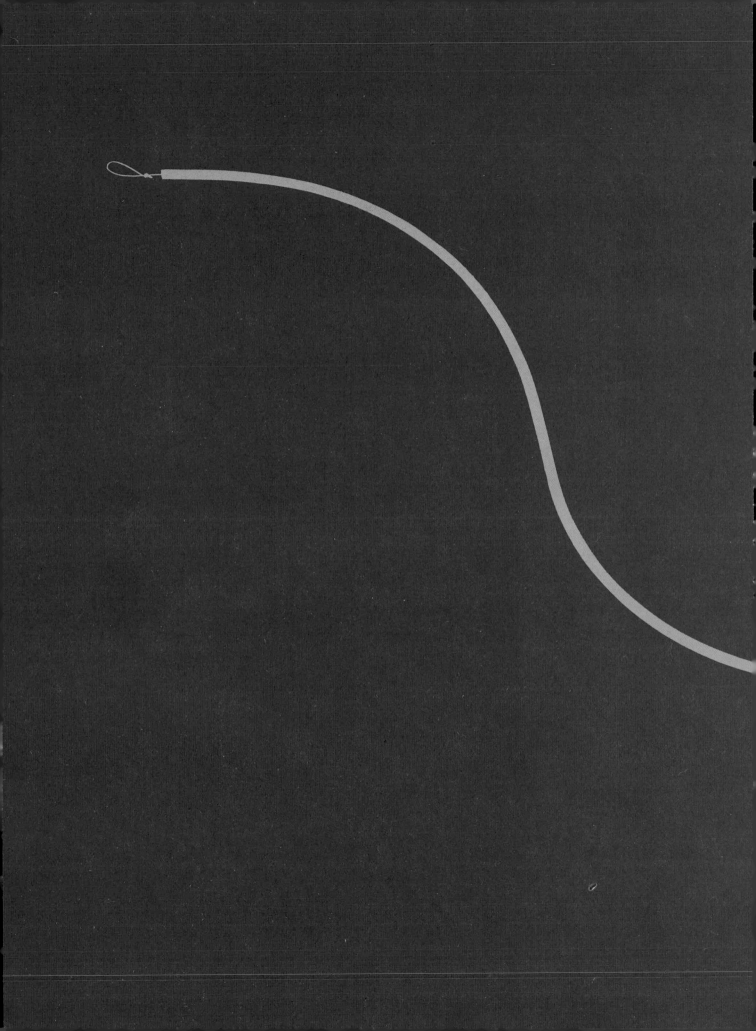

Safe & Simple
Projects With Electricity

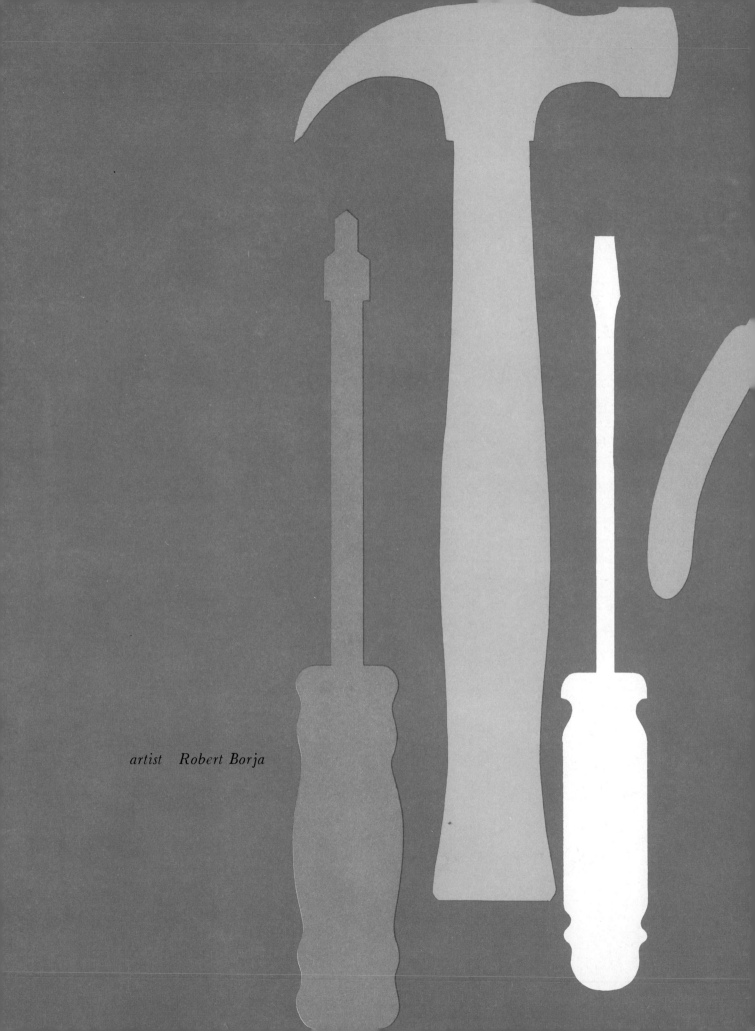

artist   Robert Borja

SAFE & SIMPLE PROJECTS WITH

Electricity

by Charles D. Neal, Ed. D., Professor of Teacher Education,
Southern Illinois University, Carbondale

CHILDRENS PRESS · Chicago

Contents

Copyright © 1965, Childrens Press
All rights reserved. Printed in the U.S.A.
Published simultaneously in Canada
Library of Congress Catalog Card Number: 65-12228

2 3 4 5 6 7 8 9 10 11 12 13 14 15 16 17 18 19 20 21 22 23 24 25   R   75 74 73 72 71 70 69 68 67

This is a book about electricity, but not one that only talks about it. Rather, it is a book of practical, easy projects. As you build these things, step by step, you will see and understand what makes each one work.

Would you like to see a coil of wire and a magnet set up an electric current? Would you like to make a hot dog cooker? Electric motor? Electric bell? Fire alarm? Burglar alarm?

Would you like to see how chemists use electricity and electroplate a nail?

Most of the projects in this book call for only the usual materials and tools found around the home.

Foreword

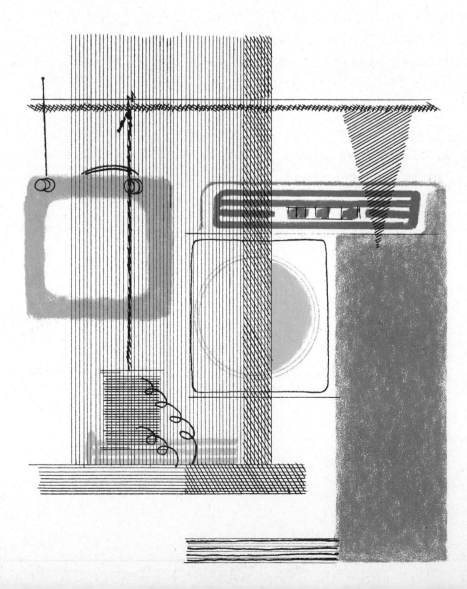

The other equipment you will need costs very little and can be secured easily from the sources mentioned.

You can have great fun making and using the things in this book. More than this, you will begin to understand how electricity travels, how it produces light and heat, how it can be used to work for us and how it carries messages.

As you do the things suggested here, you will begin to see for yourself why electricity is so important in our way of life. You will also understand why a further advancement in electricity will make ours an easier and better world in which to live. Since the advancement in uses of electricity will be made by our scientists of tomorrow, perhaps you are just the one to move into bigger and better things electrically when you finish with this book. If you have the will to do it, you can. Remember, Thomas A. Edison was once a child who, at one time, knew very little about electricity. Yet he lived to become one of our greatest men in the field.

Begin working on the projects as soon as you can. Work carefully and follow the directions and pictures exactly as given. If you don't always succeed at first, try, try, again. Remember, those who reach the moon, first must learn to fly through space. As you do succeed, you will take great pride in your own projects. And you will have a lot of fun working on them.

Definitions of some of the words in this book

Armature
usually an iron core fixed on a spindle with conductors wound around it and attached to the commutator

Bell wire
light, insulated copper wire

Carbon
an element which is often used as the cathode in a battery

Circuit
an arrangement along which moving electrons can be controlled and used to work

Commutator
a device for reversing the direction of an electric current

Conductor
the kind of material with a large number of free electrons that may be moved from atom to atom (such as most metals)

Dry cell battery
one in which the electrolyte unit is paste instead of liquid

Electromagnet
an iron core with insulated wire wound around it which becomes a magnet only when connected to a source of electricity

Electroplating
The process of coating a metal by electrical means

Electrons
negative particles of an atom that become electric current when the flow of them is directed through a conductor

Filament
threadlike conductor that gives off light or heat when electric current is passed through it

Fuse
a safety device in an electric circuit in which the metal melts

and breaks the circuit when the current increases beyond safe strength

Galvanized
coated with zinc

Galvanometer
an instrument for detecting or measuring a small amount of electric current

Generator
a machine which changes mechanical energy into electrical energy

Insulator
material within which free electrons cannot be moved easily

Kilowatt
1000 watts

Mercury
a heavy metal in liquid state at ordinary temperatures

Meter
a measuring device

Socket
a convenient device with which an appliance can be connected to the electrical power

Switch
a device for making and breaking connections in an electric circuit

Terminal
something attached to the end of an electric wire for ease in making connections

Volt
unit of electromotive force

Watt
a practical unit for measuring the rate of work

History

When Benjamin Franklin flew his kite in a storm in 1752, and proved that lightning was electricity, he knew something about this strange force in nature, but not much.

He knew that in 600 B.C. a Greek scientist had rubbed a piece of amber with cloth and produced enough electricity to attract a feather. He knew that in the following two thousand years scientists in many countries had built friction machines to make electricity. They had discovered a way to store it in a jar with water in it. They had found that electricity would travel through some things and not through others.

Knowing these things, Franklin put a metal rod on the tip of a kite. If lightning were electricity, as he believed it was, it would flow through the metal rod and down the wet string to the metal key. By standing under a shelter so that he could keep the silk ribbon at the end of his string dry, he would have a nonconductor to hold on to. He proved his point. He captured some electricity and stored it in a jar.

About this time, scientists in many parts of the world were beginning to work with the flow of electricity, with current, and they were trying to find better ways of producing electricity.

An Italian named Volta produced a steady flow of electricity with a pile of copper and zinc plates with pads, soaked in acid or salt solution, between them.

Michael Faraday, an English chemist, experimented with magnets to make electricity and discovered the working basis for an electric generator.

Once electrical power could be produced and stored and put to work, invention followed invention.

Now electricity lights cities, provides heat, moves trains, carries messages, runs machines, powers tools and serves man in countless ways.

What seems to be a perfectly innocent piece of wire may have electrons flowing through it called an electric current. Such an electric current can be as harmless as that found in a lighted flashlight. Or it can be as deadly as that found in a high voltage power line.

Open, closed, and short circuits

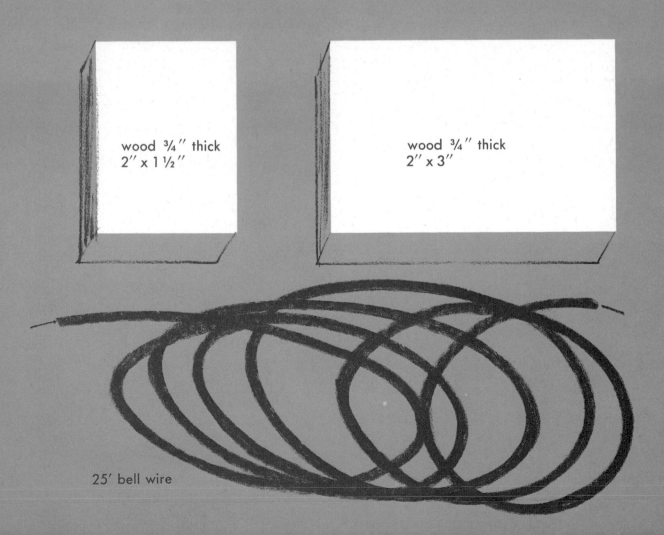

wood ¾″ thick
2″ x 1 ½″

wood ¾″ thick
2″ x 3″

25′ bell wire

How can you tell when a wire is safe to handle? The fact is, you generally cannot at first glance. For you cannot see electricity. Neither can you smell it. But many times you can feel it. By the time you feel it, you may be dead. This is the danger of playing with high voltage electricity. CAUTION: Never handle any wire until you are sure where each end is connected.

The following project, making use of open, closed, and short circuits, deals with *low voltage electricity*. Here the current flow is at a safe level. There is not the slightest danger, providing you do not go beyond the given instructions. This is also true of the remaining projects. Safety measures are carefully explained, even where regular house voltage of 110-120 volts is involved as in some of the projects. If safety measures are not taken, house current can be very dangerous.

What you need:

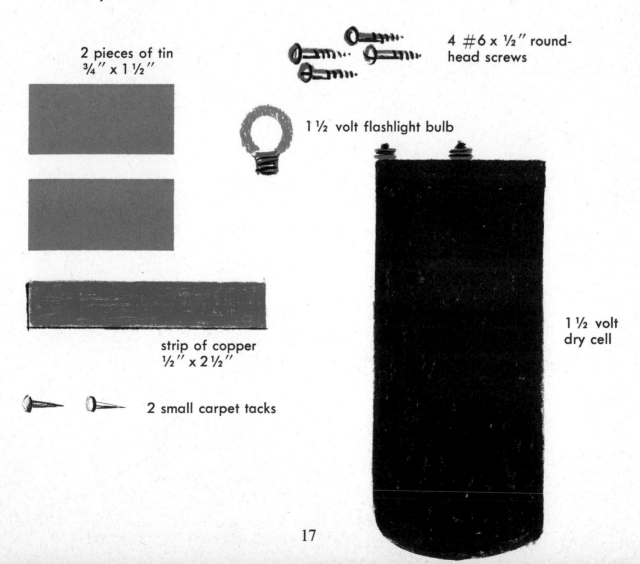

2 pieces of tin
¾″ x 1½″

4 #6 x ½″ round-head screws

1½ volt flashlight bulb

strip of copper
½″ x 2½″

1½ volt dry cell

2 small carpet tacks

Screw the flashlight bulb into the socket. You may buy a porcelain socket or you can make your own.

If you decide to make your own socket, begin by drilling an 11/16″ hole in a piece of tin with a metal bit as shown.

Now bend the piece of tin into an L shape.

Next bend the second piece of tin exactly the same way.

Using the two carpet tacks, fasten the two L-shaped pieces of tin 3/16″ apart on the 1½″ x 2″ block of wood. Be sure to drive the carpet tacks near the edge of the tin L's as shown. Round corners with tin snips or a file.

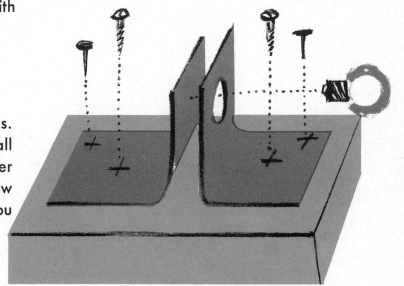

Two brass screws serve as terminals. Using a hammer and a nail, make a small hole next to each carpet tack in the center of each L. Fasten the screws in place. Now you have a socket. Save your socket. You will use it again in future projects.

You can also make your own switch. Fasten one of the screws in the center and ½″ from the edge of the ¾″ x 2″ x 3″ scrap of wood.

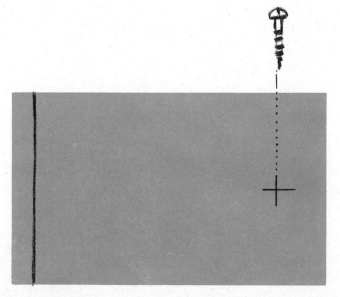

Make a bend in the copper strip. Then using the remaining screw, fasten one end of the copper strip in the center and near the edge of the piece of wood. Your switch is now complete.

CAUTION: It is dangerous to connect this switch to high voltage, such as your house circuit.

Save your switch. You will use it again in future projects.

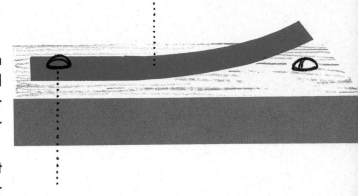

Screw the flashlight bulb into the socket, being certain it makes good contact. (Store socket shown.)

Now using short pieces of bell wire, connect the dry cell, switch, and socket together.

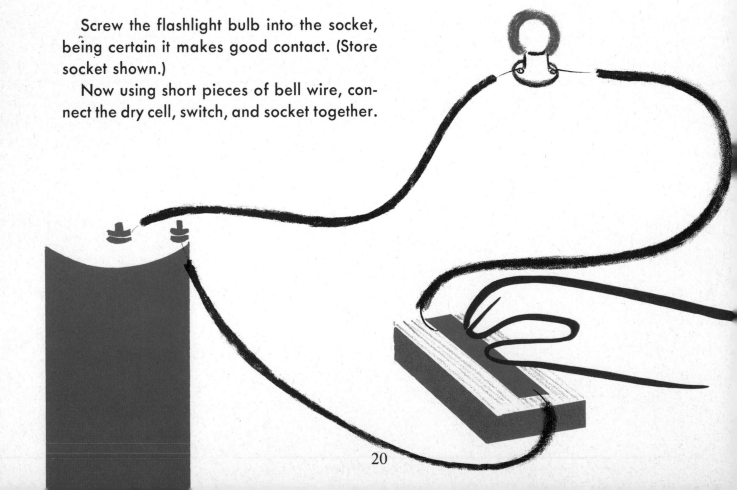

Be sure to strip the insulation from each end of a connecting wire.

If you have made all the connections right, the light burns when you press the switch. The switch acts as a gate. When it is closed, the circuit is complete. The electrons flow from the battery through the switch and flashlight bulb and return to the battery. When a switch is closed the electrons can travel and return to a starting point, we call this a *closed circuit*.

Release the switch. Now the switch is open. There is a gap in the circuit. The electrons cannot flow, so the light cannot burn. This is called an *open circuit*.

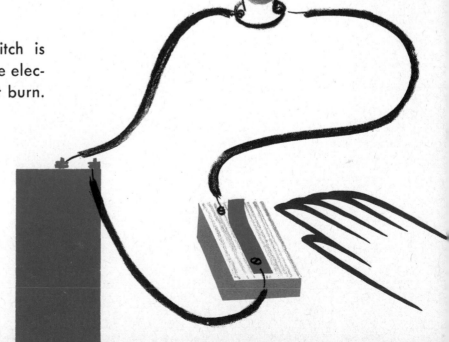

Again close the switch. This time hold it in place with a heavy object such as a book. Remove the insulation from the ends of a short piece of bell wire. Touch each end to a socket terminal. You have just made a short cut for the electrons to travel, and most of them will go that way. The wire will get warm and the light will go out. This is called a *short circuit*. CAUTION: A short circuit is very hard on your dry cell. So touch the short circuit wire to the socket terminals for just a moment at a time.

Sometimes other conductors such as extra wires or metal tools accidently make a short circuit in house wiring. Then the wires get so hot, a fuse in the fuse box melts. When this happens, a gap is automatically made, causing an open circuit. This stops the flow of electrons, preventing the wires from getting red hot. Correctly sized fuses save many homes from burning when a short circuit occurs. Since a fuse is a protective device, a penny or other piece of metal should never be put behind it.

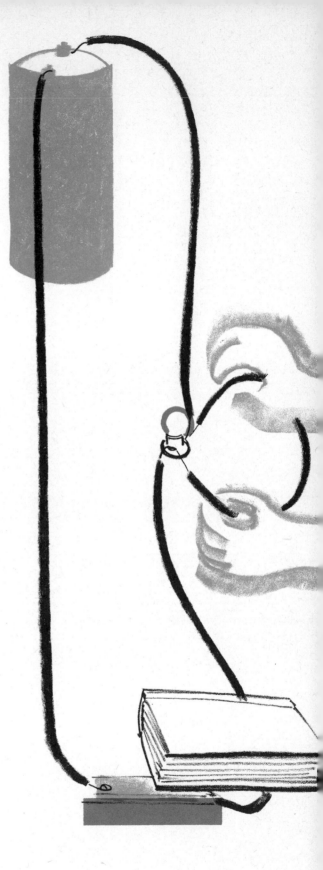

When an electrical or an electronics engineer designs a new piece of equipment, he is faced with many questions, and must have the right answers for them. One question, however, is basic: Shall the circuit be wired in parallel or in series?

Parallel
& series
circuits

Here you will discover the difference between circuits wired in parallel and those wired in series. You will also learn *how* to wire them and *why* they are different.

What you need:

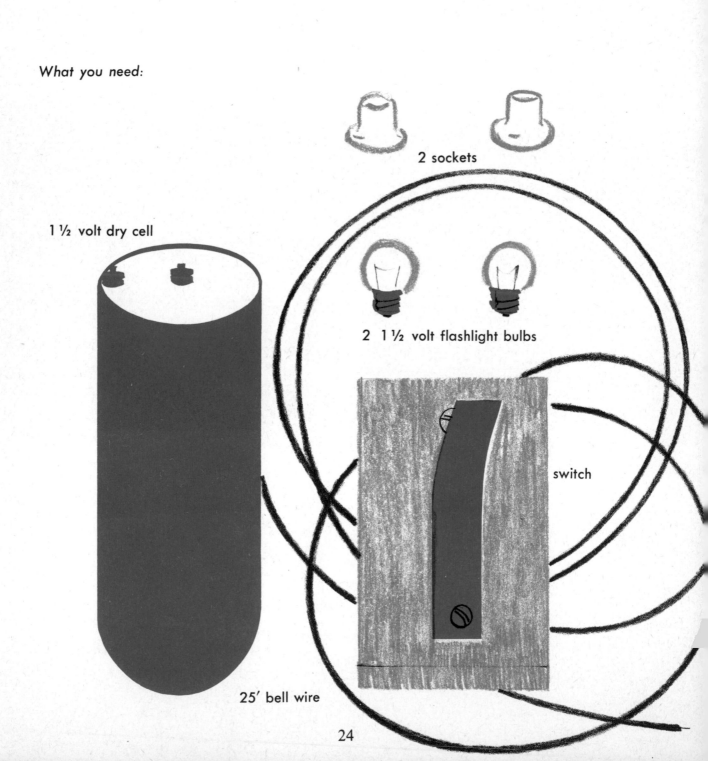

2 sockets

1 ½ volt dry cell

2 1 ½ volt flashlight bulbs

switch

25' bell wire

You can use all the parts described in the previous project. In addition, you will need to make or buy a second socket.

Screw the flashlight bulbs into the sockets. Be sure they make good contact.

Using short pieces of bell wire, hook up the dry cell, switch and two sockets as shown.

Pressing the switch should cause both lights to burn dimly.

This is called a circuit wired in *series*.

Closing the switch, unscrew one of the lights. Notice both lights go out? Since *all* of the current passes through each socket, the lights go out because the circuit is not complete.

Old-fashioned Christmas tree lights were connected in series. When one light bulb burned out, all the lights went out.

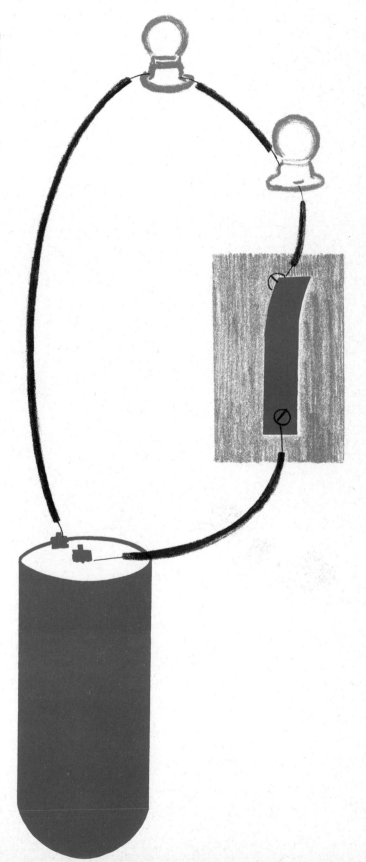

Now using bell wire, hook up the dry cell, switch and two sockets as shown. This is called a *parallel* wired circuit.

Closing the switch, unscrew one of the lights. Surprised that the second light burns? A light in a parallel circuit continues to burn even if one or more lights are burned out or removed.

The reason for this is easy to explain. In a parallel circuit, the current is divided. Some electrons can flow through one of the bulbs and some can flow through the other. Unscrewing one bulb only opens the circuit for that one light. The others still have electrons flowing through them and continue to burn.

Notice how bright both lights burn when the switch is closed? Lights wired in parallel burn brighter than those wired in series.

House lights are hooked up in parallel circuits.

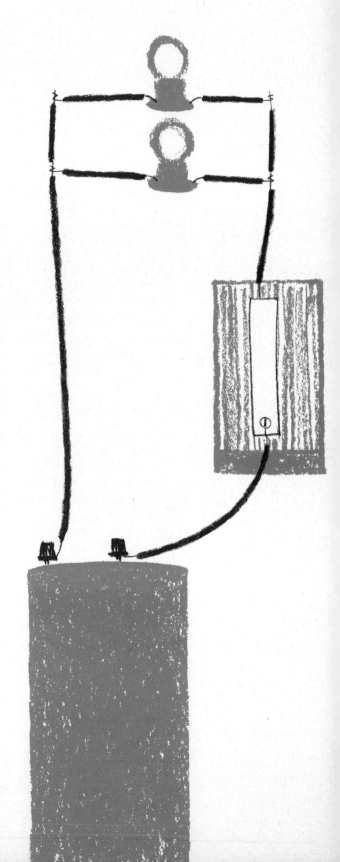

Have you ever wondered why it is possible to turn lights on at one doorway and turn them off at another? Perhaps you discovered this can be done regardless of which door you enter first. And this is correct.

Lights or other electrical appliances turned on and off from different places

The secret lies in the use of several two-way and three-way switches. With circuits wired through such switches it is possible to turn on and off lights or electric appliances from many different places.

This project will let you see exactly how a two-way switch works. Here you will be able to show your friends how to turn on and off a light from two different places.

What you need:

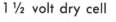
1 ½ volt dry cell

2 two-way switches

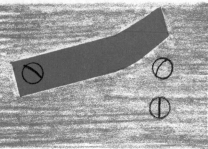

1 ½ volt flashlight bulb

socket

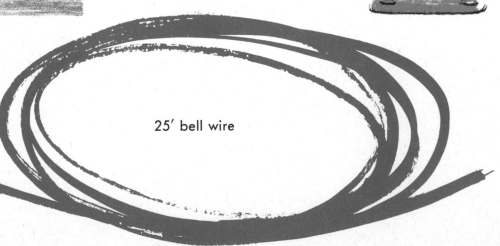
25' bell wire

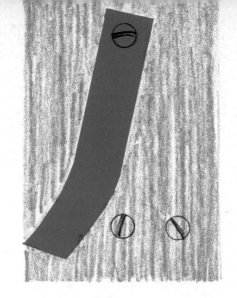

You will need all the parts mentioned in project one. In addition, you will need to make a second switch as described.

The switches you now have are called one way.

It is easy to change your one-way switches to two-way. Screw an additional #6 x ½″ roundhead screw near the edge of the block. Be sure the copper strip can be turned to make contact with it. For this screw becomes the second terminal, which is required of all two-way switches.

Be sure the light bulb makes good contact in the socket.

Using short pieces of bell wire, connect the dry cell, socket, and two switches as shown.

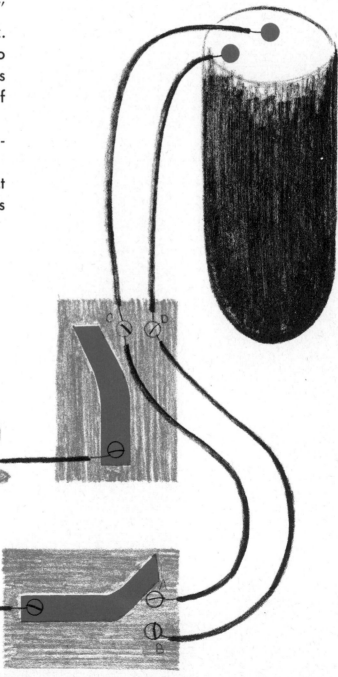

The operation of the light from either switch depends on whether the switch opens or closes the circuit.

When switch #1 makes contact with point A and switch #2 makes contact with point D, the current travels through the circuit. This causes the light to burn because the circuit is completed.

The circuit is also completed when switch #1 makes contact with point B and switch #2 makes contact with point C. These two circuit possibilities make it practical to turn the light on or off from two different locations.

You can demonstrate this project with the switches located some distance apart. Simply use a heavy non-metal object, such as a book, to hold one of the copper strips on the proper contact point while you operate the second switch. You can also have a friend operate one switch while you operate the other one.

You know that a switch is used to open and close a circuit. But sometimes it is hard to understand how this takes place. With the mercury switch you can see what really happens. And you will find many other uses for it. One such use is in the project where you learn how to make a burglar alarm. Besides putting the switch to many good uses, you will be able to show your friends what happens when it opens and closes a circuit.

Mercury switch

What you need:

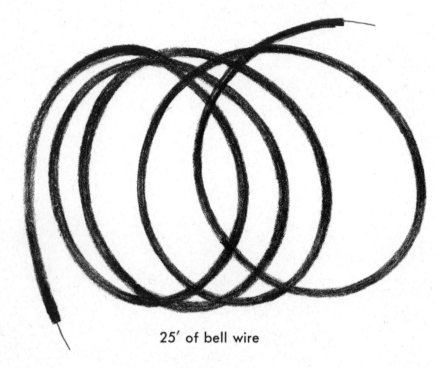

25' of bell wire

1 ½ volt dry cell

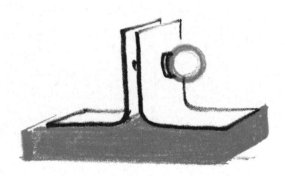

flashlight bulb and socket
(homemade socket shown)

small, transparent
plastic pill
bottle with
snap-on flexible
top (A small
bufferin bottle is
a good example.)

½ teaspoonful of mercury
(May be bought
in any drugstore.)

1 roll of plastic
electricians' tape

32

Cut two pieces of bell wire about 8″ long. Scrape about 1″ of insulation from the ends.

Using a box-8 nail or an ice pick, punch two holes about ½″ apart in the plastic lid.

Pour the mercury into the bottle and snap the plastic lid in place. CAUTION: Mercury can tarnish jewelry. So if you are wearing a ring or wrist watch, remove them for this part of the project.

Push one end of each bell wire piece through a hole. The wires should be parallel with each other and the ends should be about ⅛″ from the bottom of the bottle.

Bend the wires down across the lid and about halfway down the side of the bottle. Hold them in place with two turns of plastic tape wrapped around the bottle.

Using short bell wire pieces, connect the dry cell, the socket and bulb, and the mercury switch in series as shown.

The secret of the switch lies in its mounting angle. The lamp burns because the mercury is in position to carry electrons from one wire to the other. Now tilt the bottle as shown below. Notice the mercury is no longer making contact with both wires. When the mercury does not make proper contact, the light goes out. It goes out because the circuit is open.

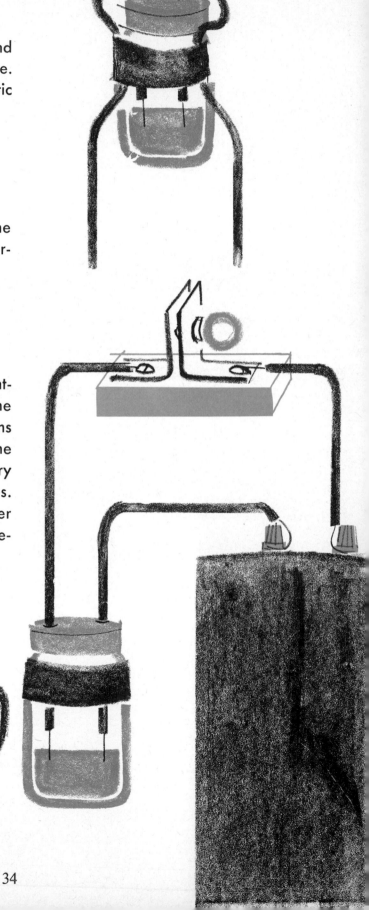

Electronics have moved into the schoolroom. More and more schools are using electronic teaching machines to help do a better job of teaching. Perhaps you have used one of these machines. Did you know that you can make a teaching machine? The one described here is easy to make. You can have a lot of fun making up questions and answers from this book. Then see how many questions your friends can answer correctly when they use your teaching machine.

Teaching machine

2

1 ? no

4

5 what is the

3

when

6 yes

A B series

0

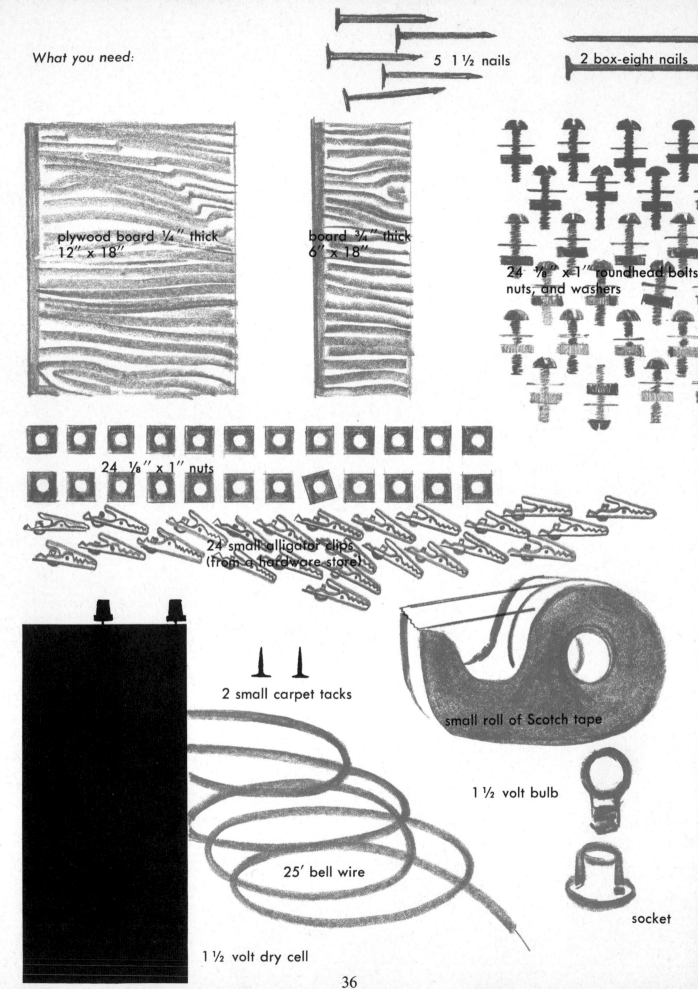

What you need:

5 1 ½ nails

2 box-eight nails

plywood board ¼" thick
12" x 18"

board ¾" thick
6" x 18"

24 ⅛" x 1" roundhead bolts,
nuts, and washers

24 ⅛" x 1" nuts

24 small alligator clips
(from a hardware store)

2 small carpet tacks

small roll of Scotch tape

1 ½ volt bulb

25' bell wire

socket

1 ½ volt dry cell

Using the 5 1½ nails, fasten the two boards together as shown.

With a pencil draw two vertical lines on the large board. Also mark off 12 short, horizontal lines ¾″ apart on each vertical line.

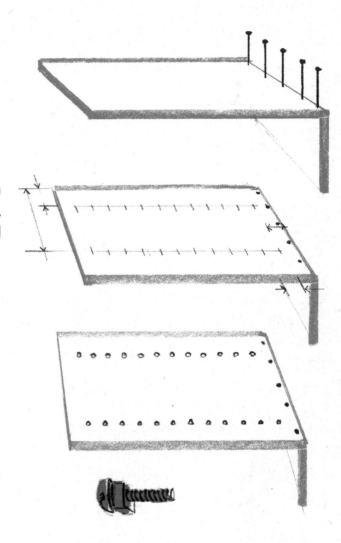

Using an ⅛″ bit, drill 24 holes where the vertical and horizontal lines cross.

Screw the 24 additional nuts tight against the heads of the 24 bolts.

Now bring the 24 bolts up from the bottom through the top board. Place a washer over each bolt and tighten in place with a nut. The spaces alongside the bolts on the left side are used for questions, while those on the right side are used for answers.

Cut 12 lengths of bell wire, each about 20″ long. Strip the insulation from the ends of each wire.

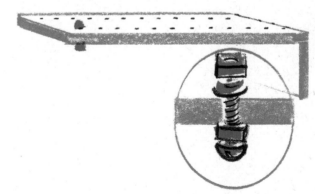

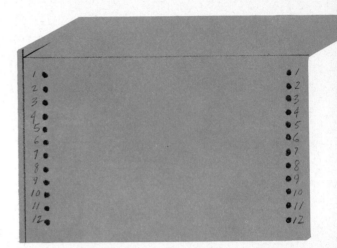

Fasten the end of each strip of bell wire to an alligator clip.

Turn the board over so the heads of the bolts face you. This is the back of the board. Number the holes on each vertical line from 1 to 12.

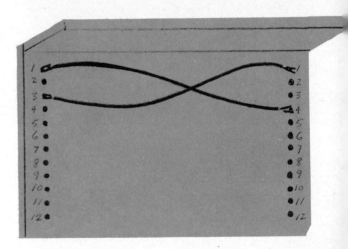

Now crisscross pairs of bolts by clamping the clips onto the bolt heads, always going from a "question" bolt to an "answer" bolt. The picture shows how this is done. Changing the wiring frequently will prevent those who use the machine from memorizing "right" bolts rather than correct answers.

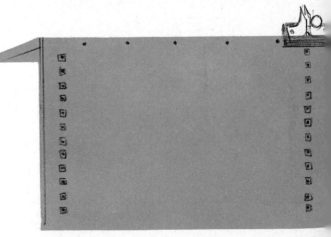

Turn the board over, right side up. Using two carpet tacks, fasten the socket near the upper right hand corner. This is the tin socket made in an earlier project.

Using a short piece of bell wire, connect one terminal of the socket to the dry cell.

Cut two pieces of bell wire each about 24" in length. Fasten one end of each wire securely to one of the box-8 nails.

Connect the free end of one of the pieces of bell wire to the remaining terminal on the socket. Now connect the free end of the second piece of bell wire to the remaining terminal on the dry cell. Your teaching machine is complete. Now for the question sheet.

Lay a piece of 8½" x 11" lined writing paper opposite the "question" bolts. Write the numbers 1 to 12 on the paper opposite the corresponding bolt. Do the same for the "answer" bolts.

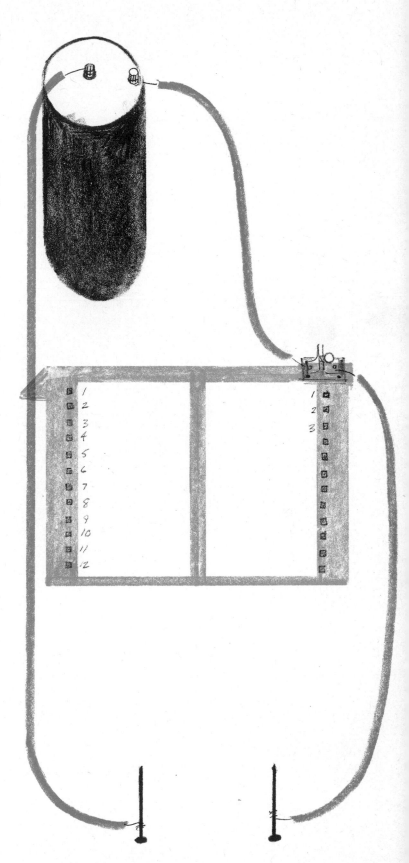

Opposite each number on the question sheet, write a question. You may want to get your questions from this book.

Now prepare your answer sheet. Be sure each answer is written opposite the number corresponding to the "answer" bolt that is connected to the right "question" bolt. For example, "question" bolt #1 and "answer" bolt #4 are connected together in the diagram on page 38.

When your question and answer sheets are complete, fasten them in place on the teaching machine with a small piece of Scotch tape. The numbers on the sheets must be opposite corresponding bolts.

To play the game, have a friend place one box-8 nail against a question bolt. Have him place the other against what he thinks is the correct "answer" bolt. If he is right, the light should flash on. (The light burns because a complete circuit is made when "question" bolts are connected to correct "answer" bolts.) Give him one point for each question scored correctly. See which one of your friends knows the most about science. CAUTION: Each time you make out a new set of questions, change the answer code by re-connecting the alligator clips to the "answer" bolts. Always be sure your answers are written according to the wiring diagram on the board.

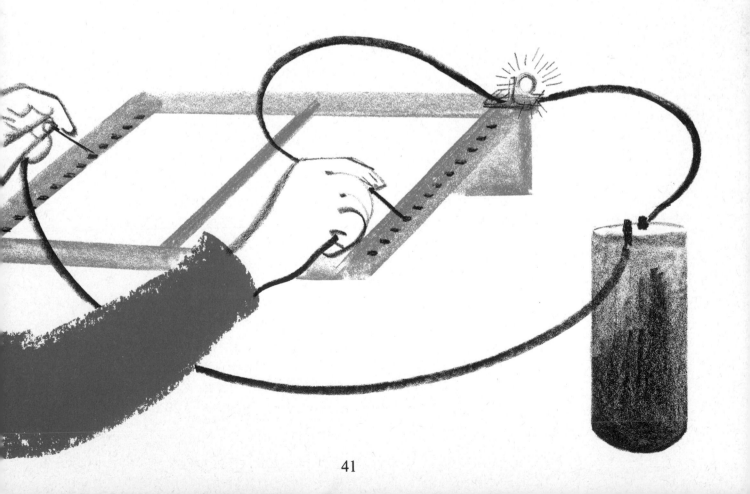

"Hockus-pocus ali kazan" sends Joe diving to the bottom. On the command, "Up," Joe quickly surfaces. Fun awaits you with the Diver Joe project. Your startled friends will watch in amazement as you magically control Joe's actions.

Magic
Diver Joe

Many magic tricks are based upon sound scientific principles, and Diver Joe is no exception. What appears to be magic is really an electromagnet attracting a small nail to the bottom of a glass of water. You will see for yourself exactly how and why this happens when your project is completed.

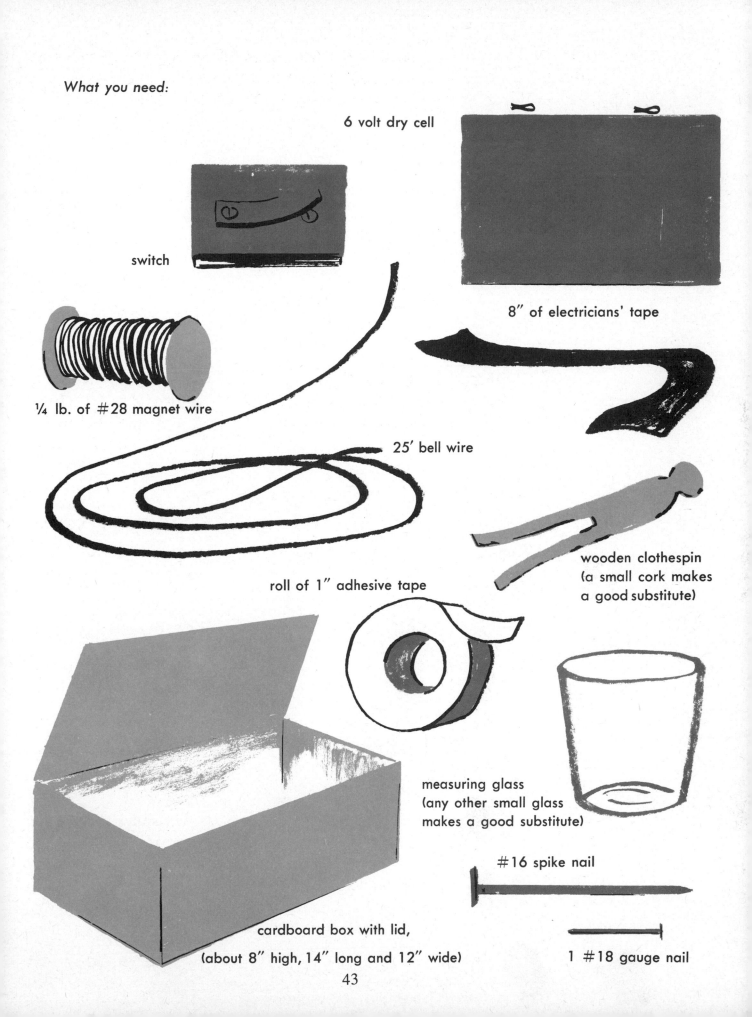

What you need:

6 volt dry cell

switch

8" of electricians' tape

¼ lb. of #28 magnet wire

25' bell wire

wooden clothespin
(a small cork makes
a good substitute)

roll of 1" adhesive tape

measuring glass
(any other small glass
makes a good substitute)

#16 spike nail

cardboard box with lid,
(about 8" high, 14" long and 12" wide)

1 #18 gauge nail

43

First wrap friction tape around the spike nail near its point as shown. Then wind the insulated #28 gauge magnet wire 600 times in the same direction around the nail. Be sure to leave about 3' of wire sticking out at the end. Twist the wires to keep the coil from unwrapping.

Strip about 1" of the insulation from the ends of the wires.

With adhesive tape fasten the electromagnet to the box. Place it so the spike head is near the middle, on the underneath side, of the cardboard box top. Be sure the box lid works from top to bottom.

Place the battery inside the box. Connect one of the lead wires from the electromagnet to one of the posts on the dry cell battery. Connect the other lead wire to a terminal on the switch. Using bell wire, connect the second switch terminal to the remaining dry cell terminal.

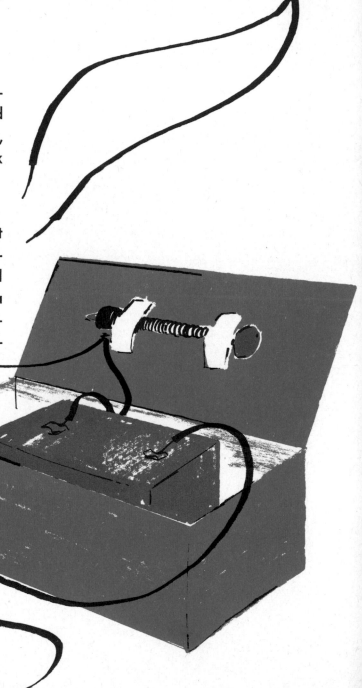

Using a back hand saw, cut ⅞" from the clothespin. Now drive the 1" nail into the middle of the clothespin for about ¼".

Paint Diver Joe the color of your choice. Be sure to let the paint dry completely before continuing.

Place Joe inside the glass. Pour water into the glass until the nail head is about ¼" from the bottom. Then place the center of the glass directly

over the spike nail head of the electromagnet. Press the switch, and release it quickly. Watch Diver Joe quickly dive, then surface! If Diver Joe fails to respond, remove some water from the glass. (An electromagnet is limited as to the distance it will attract iron, removing water should increase its strength.)

Here is what actually happens. When you press or close the switch, a complete circuit is made. This activates the electromagnet, causing it to pull downward on the small nail. Diver Joe has no other choice but to go down with the nail. When you release the switch, the circuit is broken, or opened, and Diver Joe surfaces.

Perhaps you have noticed people using different kinds of meters when they work with electricity. Yes, auto mechanics, radio-T.V. repairmen, and electrical scientists all use meters of one kind or another in their work.

Electric current detector or galvanometer

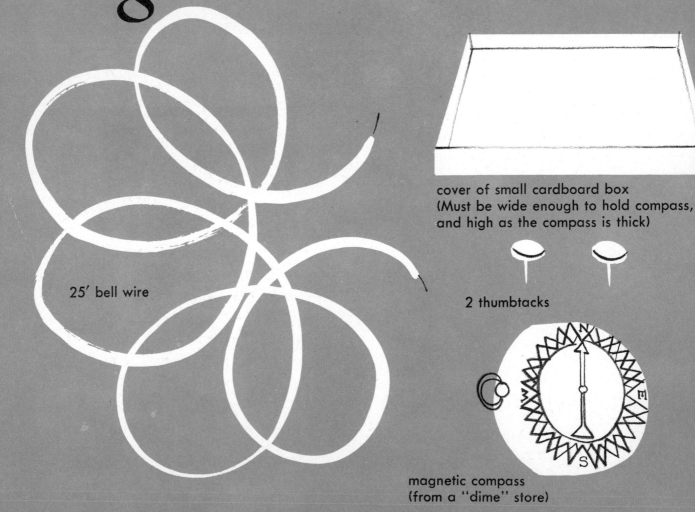

25' bell wire

cover of small cardboard box (Must be wide enough to hold compass, and high as the compass is thick)

2 thumbtacks

magnetic compass (from a "dime" store)

Did you know you can make a meter that will serve a useful purpose? You can. It is called an *electric current detector* or *galvanometer*. It will tell you if an electric current is present. Since electricity cannot be seen, it is important to have such a meter to tell us if a battery is dead or whether an electric current is flowing through a circuit. CAUTION: A galvanometer should be used only where you think a small quantity of electricity is present. Otherwise, the galvanometer can be destroyed.

What you need:

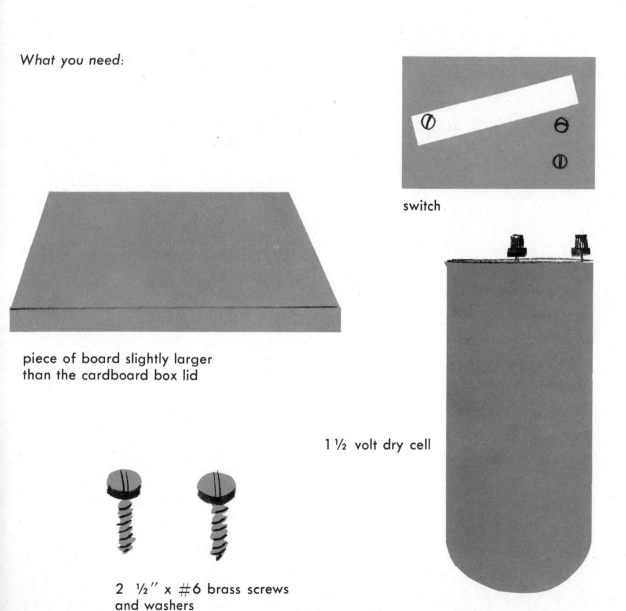

switch

piece of board slightly larger
than the cardboard box lid

1 ½ volt dry cell

2 ½″ x #6 brass screws
and washers

Place the magnetic compass in the box.

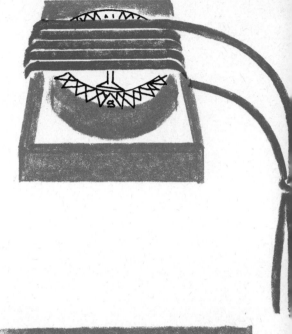

Wrap about 20 turns of bell wire in the same direction around the box cover. Leave about 3 inches of wire sticking out on each end.

Using the two thumbtacks, fasten the box lid to the piece of board as shown. This holds the coil of wire securely in place.

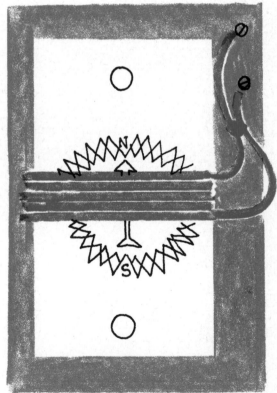

Scrape the insulation from the ends of the coil wires. Using the two brass screws and washers, fasten the wires in place as shown. Do not turn the screws down tight. This completes your current detector or galvanometer.

Using bell wire, connect the dry cell to the switch.

Connect one terminal of the electric current detector to the switch with bell wire. Likewise, connect the other terminal to the dry cell. Tighten both terminal screws on the detector as well as those on the switch and the battery.

Notice, when the switch is closed, the compass needle moves. This happens because when electricity moves through a coil of wire, magnetism is all around it. This magnetism goes through the glass to the magnetic needle and moves it. So any time you connect your electric current detector to a circuit or a battery, you have an electric current if the needle moves. If it does not move, there is no electric current present.

In addition to testing circuits and batteries for electric current, you can also test flashlight, radio, and transistor radio batteries. Dead batteries are quickly discovered because the needle does not move.

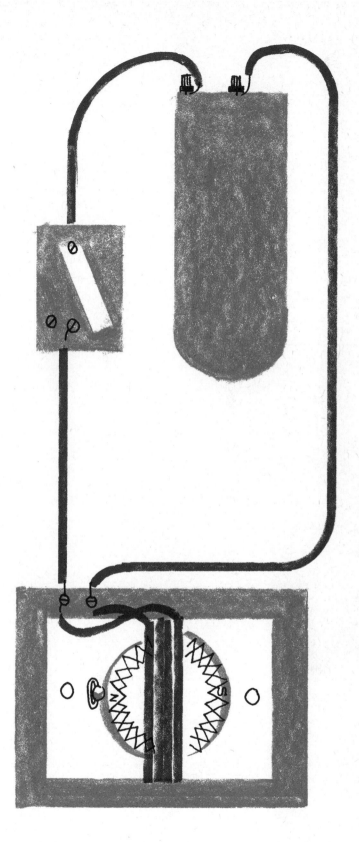

Where does an electric current come from? An electric current is nothing more than a flow of electrons. Perhaps you know that friction is one way to make electrons move. And if we rub things hard enough, we can generate some electricity. However, we cannot generate enough electricity in this way to meet our needs. Scientists have discovered other ways to generate electricity.

Wet cell battery

bell wire

old 1 ½ volt dry cell

Did you know that one way to generate electricity is from chemical action? Some people will tell you that electricity is stored inside a battery. But this is not true.

In general, there are two kinds of batteries. Both of these generate electricity from chemical action. In both batteries, chemicals act on two different kinds of metals.

A dry cell battery is actually not dry at all. It is made up of moist chemicals, a carbon rod, and a zinc cover. These are the kind of batteries found inside flashlights and portable radios.

A wet cell battery is made up of liquid chemicals and two different metals. This is true in some part of the wet cell battery in your automobile and the wet cell battery you are about to make.

What you need:

galvanometer

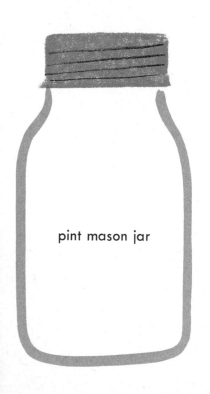
pint mason jar

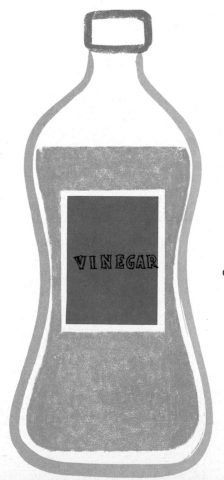
VINEGAR

acetic acid vinegar

Begin by breaking apart the old dry cell.

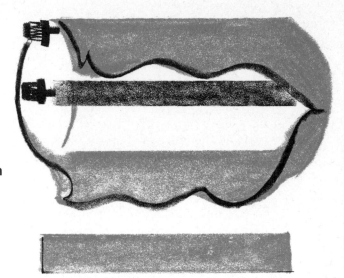

Cut a strip of zinc about ¾" x 5" from the container.

Remove the carbon rod from the dry cell. If you do not have an old dry cell, use a ¾" x 5" strip of copper in place of the carbon rod. Both the copper and the zinc strips can be bought at a hardware store.

Pour the vinegar into the jar to within about one inch from the top.

Bend a lip on one end of the zinc strip. Then place it in the jar so it hangs over the jar edge. Now place the carbon rod in the jar. Make sure the carbon rod and zinc strip do not touch each other. You have just made a wet cell battery.

Using bell wire, connect the switch and galvanometer together. Be sure to fasten a second piece of bell wire to the switch and to the galvanometer as shown.

Now connect the loose ends of the wires from the switch and galvanometer to the zinc strip and carbon rod. Be sure your connections are clean and tight.

Close the circuit by pressing the switch. The electric current generated should be strong enough to register on your galvanometer.

The electric current was generated because a chemical action took place. This chemical action caused the carbon rod to develop a shortage of electrons. At the same time it caused the zinc strip to develop an oversupply of electrons.

Because of this difference in the charges, the oversupply of electrons traveled through the circuit from the zinc strip to the carbon rod, which had fewer electrons. This flow of electrons through circuits is what scientists call an electric current.

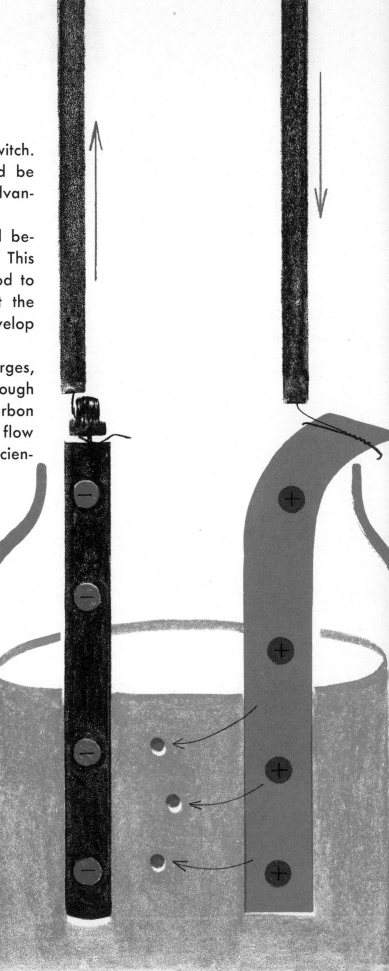

Had you ever thought that electricity from a dry cell could be used to copperplate objects made of metal? Such a way of coating one metal with another is called *electroplating*.

This project is a fascinating one. Here you will actually see a chemical change take place before your eyes.

Electroplating device

What you need:

Blue vitriol (copper sulfate) usually comes in large crystals, which may be hard to dissolve. So they should be prepared in one of two ways:

1. Have your druggist grind the crystals into a powder with a mortar and pestle or

2. Place them in a small, clean sack or wrap them in a clean cloth. Then crush them with a hammer.

strip of copper (from a hardware store)

2 tablespoons of blue vitriol (copper sulfate is the chemical name. Can be bought from any drugstore.)

box-8 nail or any large clean nail

25' bell wire

pint milk bottle or a glass about the same size

1 ½ volt dry cell

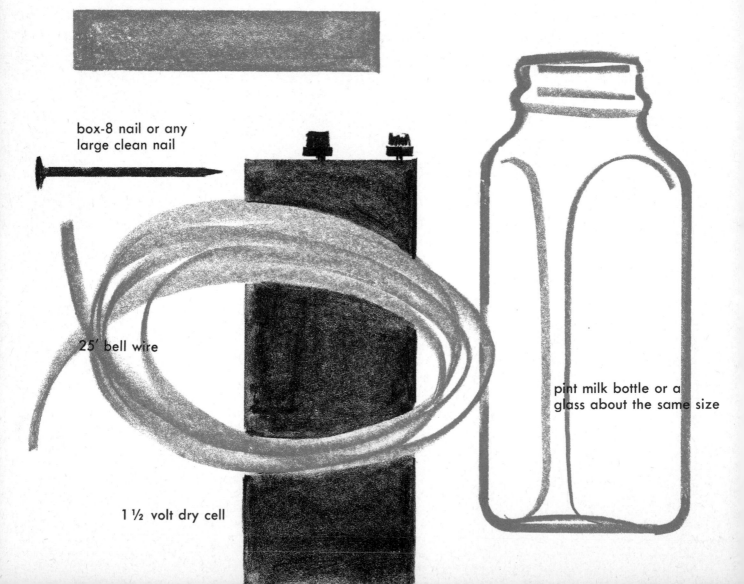

Begin by placing the two tablespoons of blue vitriol (copper sulfate) in the milk bottle almost full of warm water. Stir with a clean stick until all the crystals are dissolved. The water should now be deep blue in color. CAUTION: Blue vitriol is poisonous. Do not eat any of it. If you touch it, there is no danger if you wash your hands. To be perfectly safe, ask your father, mother, or teacher to help you with this project.

Using a small nail, punch a hole near one end of the copper strip. Also bend this end into a lip so it will hang over the edge of the milk bottle.

Using bell wire, connect one end to the positive (center) post of the dry cell. Run the end through the hole in the copper strip. Now wrap the end of the wire tightly around the copper strip. Place the strip of copper into the milk bottle.

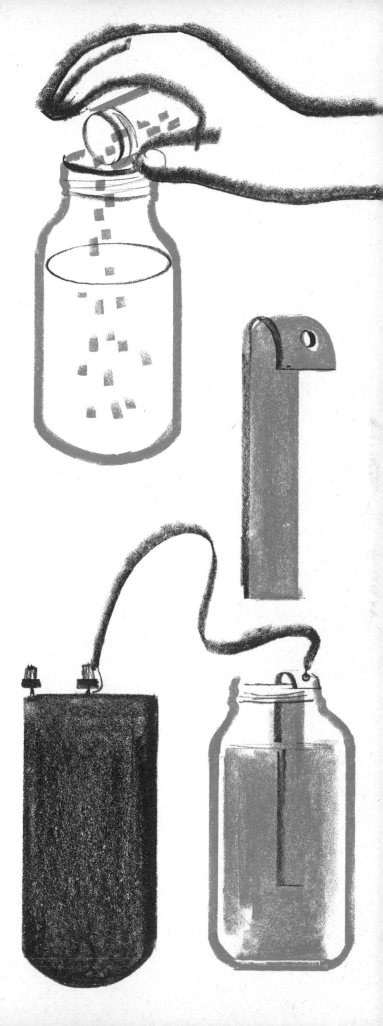

Next prepare the nail. It must be free of rust, grease and dirt. Clean the nail by sanding it. Follow up by giving it a good cleaning with soap and water.

Using a second piece of bell wire, connect one end to the negative (outside) post of the dry cell. Connect the other end of the bell wire to the nail. Wrap it a couple of turns tightly around the nail. Now place it in the milk bottle opposite the copper strip. Keep the copper strip from touching the nail.

What happens after a short while? Notice the nail becoming copper colored. It is becoming copperplated.

Where does the copperplating come from? Does it come from the copper strip? Does it come from the copper sulfate solution? Or does it come from both?

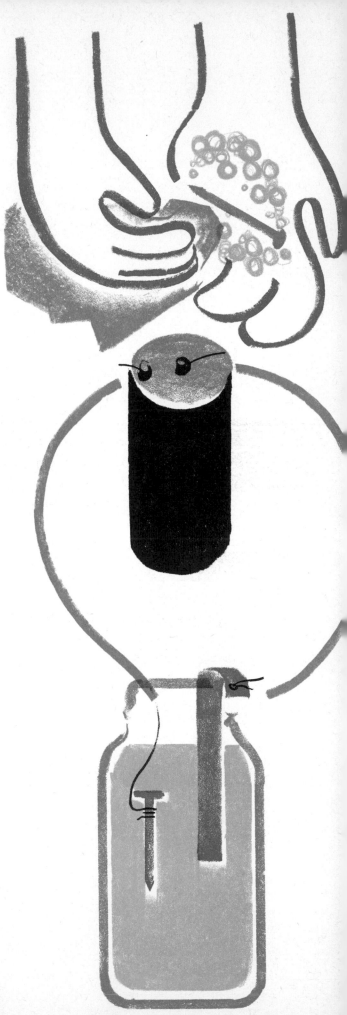

58

Here is how the chemical action took place. The copperplating on the nail came from the copper sulfate solution. As the copper atoms leave the copper sulfate for the nail, they are replaced by copper atoms that came from the copper strip.

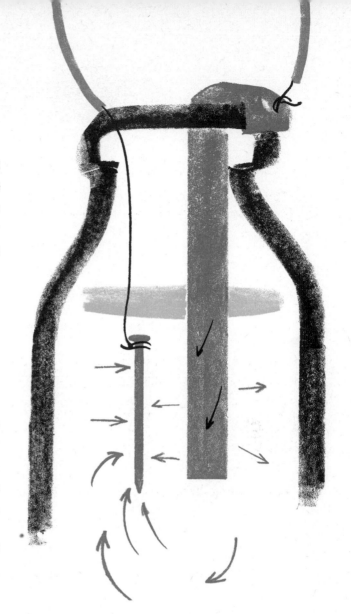

Experiment by trying to copperplate other metallic objects. You might want to try such objects as an old key or a paper clip. Be sure to give them the cleaning process as described before. Also connect them to the dry cell in the same way.

Sometimes a silver compound, a bar of silver, and an electric current are used to silver-plate knives, forks, and spoons.

Sometimes a process of gold-plating is used to cover cheap metal rings, pins, watch cases, and other jewelry.

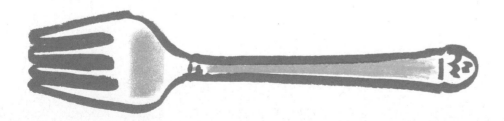

You know that some batteries generate electric current by chemical action. If this is true, you might wonder about this question: Can chemical change be brought about by electricity? If you do wonder, you are on the right track of learning about a scientific fact. For chemical change can be brought about with electricity.

Gas generator

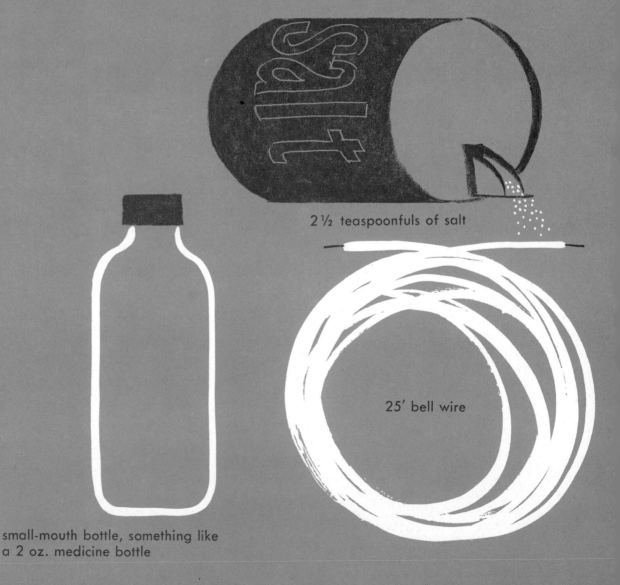

2 ½ teaspoonfuls of salt

25' bell wire

small-mouth bottle, something like a 2 oz. medicine bottle

With the gas generator described in this project, you will see exactly how this is done. In fact, you will see two gases generated by electricity before your very eyes. These are *hydrogen* and *chlorine*. Perhaps you have already become acquainted with them in other experiments. Both gases can be dangerous in large amounts. But here, only very small amounts of them can be produced. So there is no danger at all.

It is interesting to know that the principle of generating gas used in this project has real value. One such value is in the making of chlorine. It is made electrically in large commercial plants. Of course, larger and more expensive equipment is used in the process.

What you need:

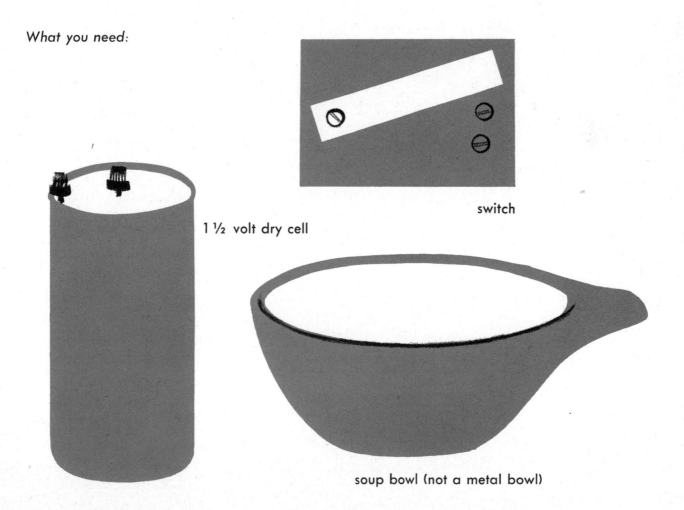

switch

1 ½ volt dry cell

soup bowl (not a metal bowl)

Cut three pieces of bell wire. Cut two pieces about 18″ long. Cut the third piece about 6″ long. Remove the insulation about 1½″ from the ends of each piece.

Use the short piece of bell wire to connect the dry cell and switch together.

Beginning at one end of each long piece of bell wire, wind about a dozen turns around a pencil. Slide the coil from the pencil. Sometimes these are called *pigtails*.

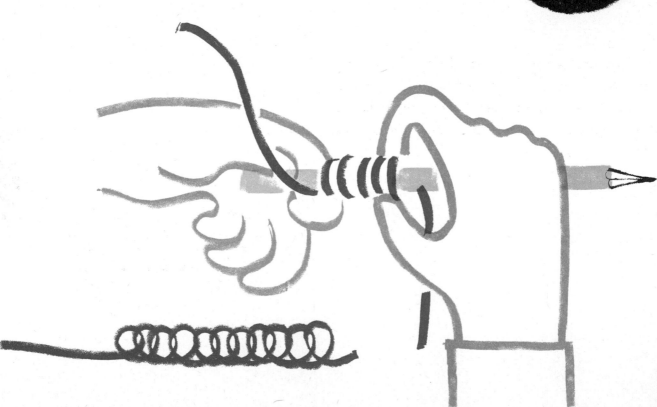

Dissolve the 2½ teaspoonfuls of salt in a glass of water. This is called a salt solution.

Fill the small medicine bottle with the salt solution. Pour the rest into the soup bowl.

Fasten one end of a pigtail wire to the switch as shown.

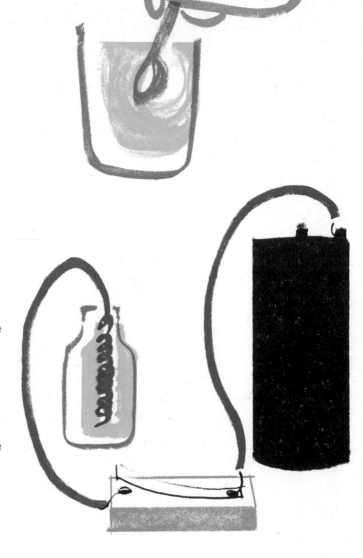

Now place the pigtail end of the wire into the medicine bottle with the solution.

Holding your thumb tightly over the mouth of the bottle, turn it upside down in the solution in the bowl. Remove your thumb while keeping the mouth of the bottle under the solution.

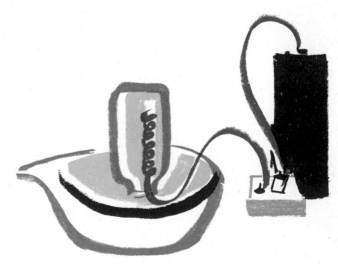

Place the second pigtail in the solution in the soup bowl. Connect the other end of the wire to the remaining battery terminal.

Press the switch. You should have a closed circuit because the salt solution completes the circuit. Notice the small bubbles leaving the pigtail in the medicine bottle? These are bubbles of hydrogen gas. Notice them collect at the top of the medicine bottle. Hydrogen is one gas that makes up water. The hydrogen gas is set free by the electric current.

What is happening at the end of the other pigtail wire? No bubbles can be seen. But after a short time, notice the end of the wire turning green. This is caused by the chlorine gas combining with the copper wire. Chlorine is one gas that makes up the salt in the solution. It is set free by the electricity. Hold the switch down until the salt solution turns a light blue. This color is also caused by the chlorine which combines with the copper.

Ever since Thomas Edison made the first incandescent light bulb, men have marvelled at his invention. It was a simple invention. Yet it was the best and most effective means of artificial light developed by mankind since the beginning of time.

Electric

light bulb

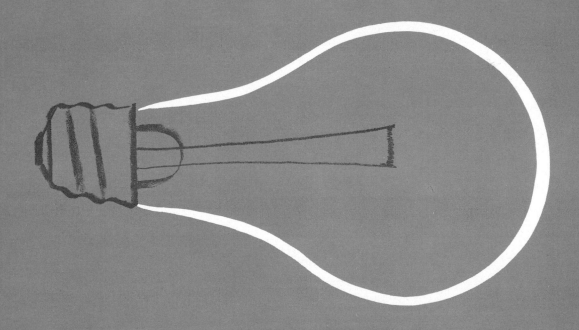

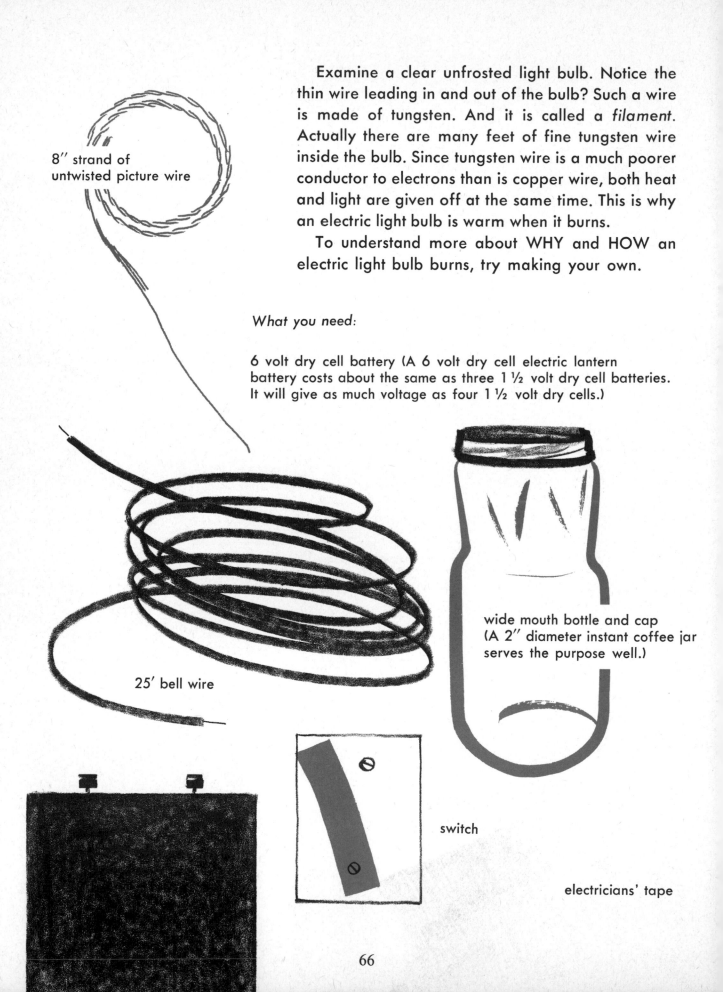

8" strand of
untwisted picture wire

Examine a clear unfrosted light bulb. Notice the thin wire leading in and out of the bulb? Such a wire is made of tungsten. And it is called a *filament*. Actually there are many feet of fine tungsten wire inside the bulb. Since tungsten wire is a much poorer conductor to electrons than is copper wire, both heat and light are given off at the same time. This is why an electric light bulb is warm when it burns.

To understand more about WHY and HOW an electric light bulb burns, try making your own.

What you need:

6 volt dry cell battery (A 6 volt dry cell electric lantern battery costs about the same as three 1 ½ volt dry cell batteries. It will give as much voltage as four 1 ½ volt dry cells.)

25' bell wire

wide mouth bottle and cap (A 2" diameter instant coffee jar serves the purpose well.)

switch

electricians' tape

66

With an ice pick or thin nail, punch two holes, about two inches apart, through the screw cap.

Strip about 1″ of insulation from one end of each of two 12″ pieces of bell wire.

Now push the pieces of bell wire through the holes for about 3″.

Next make a wire coil by wrapping the piece of the picture wire around a pencil. Leave about 1″ of wire on each end. Remove the pencil. You have just made a filament.

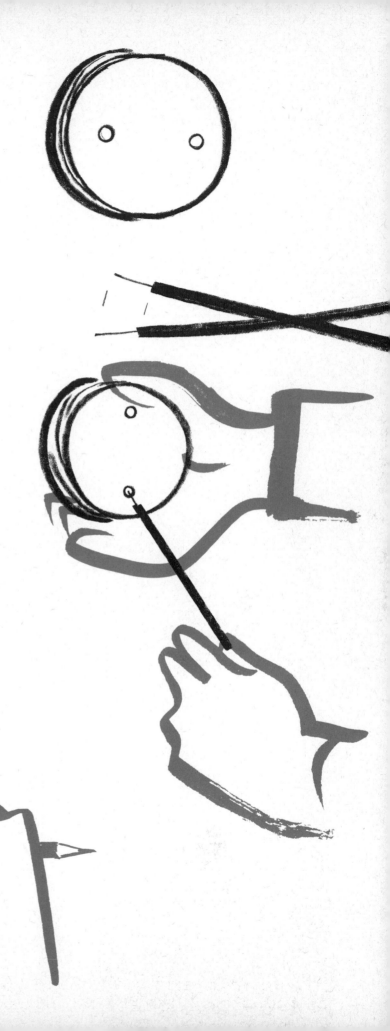

Wind the ends of the filament around the ends of the wires sticking through the cap.

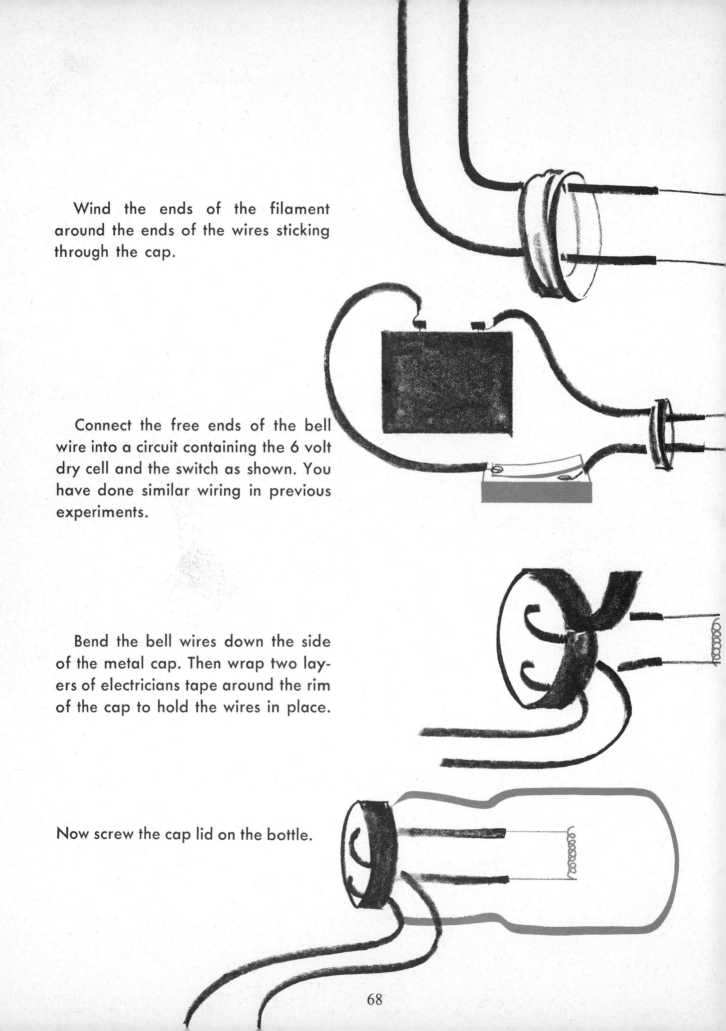

Connect the free ends of the bell wire into a circuit containing the 6 volt dry cell and the switch as shown. You have done similar wiring in previous experiments.

Bend the bell wires down the side of the metal cap. Then wrap two layers of electricians tape around the rim of the cap to hold the wires in place.

Now screw the cap lid on the bottle.

Press the switch, closing the circuit. Release the switch when the coil begins to show red. What happens when you repeat this operation several times? If your filament burns in two, this is as it should be. The reason it does is easy to explain. The oxygen in the air combines with the filament to burn it in two, thus breaking the circuit.

Because the air has been removed in a real light bulb, the filament does not burn in two for many, many hours.

Perhaps you have heard the expression, "He has nerves of steel." Perhaps you have also wondered just what this means.

Nerve machine

25' bell wire

unpainted metal curtain rod at least 3' long

2 1/8" x 3/4" round-head stove bolts, washers, and nuts

iron washer with hole slightly larger than curtain rod

1 1/2" x 6" dowel pin
(A tree limb of the same size makes a good substitute.)

With a nerve machine, you can test your own nerves to see how calm they are. You can also have a lot of fun testing the nerves of your friends. Which ones have nerves of steel? You'll learn how to answer this question when you finish making your machine.

What you need:

6 volt dry cell

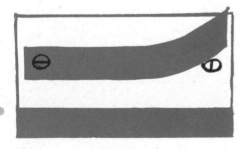

switch

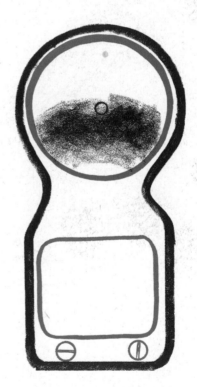

electric bell described on page 101 or regular electric door bell

Using a hammer, flatten about two inches of each end of the metal curtain rod.

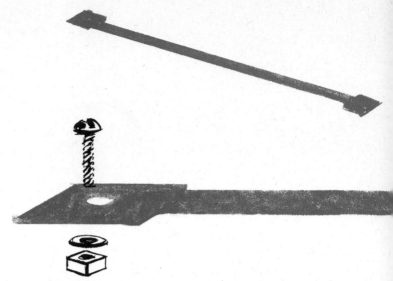

Drill a ⅛″ hole near one end of the curtain rod. Using a nut and washer, fasten one of the ⅛″ x ¾″ round-head stove bolts through the hole.

With a hand saw, cut a notch in the middle of one end of the dowel pin. The depth of the notch should be slightly less than the width of the iron washer rim.

Drill a ⅛″ hole through the middle of the notched end of the dowel pin. Be sure the hole is directly across the notch.

Drill a ⅛″ hole through the middle of the iron washer rim.

Place the iron washer in the dowel pin notch in such a way that the holes are in line. Using the second ⅛″ x ¾″ round-head stove bolt, washer and nut, fasten the washer in place. You have just made the *ring handle* for your nerve machine.

Slide the ring handle over the curtain rod. Next place the curtain rod across the backs of two chairs.

Using bell wire, connect one of the battery terminals to one of the switch terminals. Connect the second switch terminal to one of the bell terminals.

Fasten one end of a 3′ piece of bell wire to the bolt in the curtain rod. Fasten the other end to the remaining battery terminal. Next fasten a 5′ piece of bell wire to the bolt in the ring handle. Fasten the other end to the remaining bell terminal. Be sure both bolts are tight.

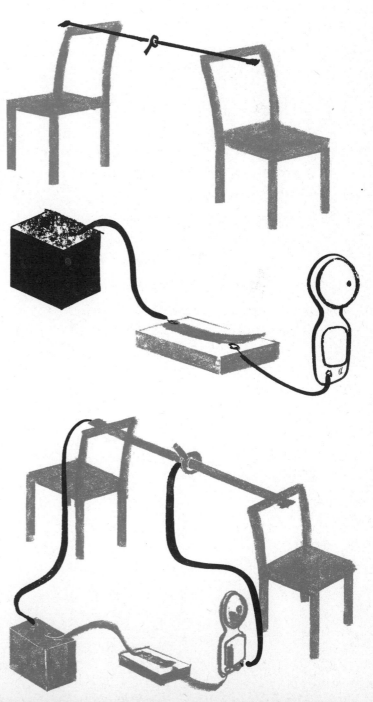

Here is the way to use your testing machine:

1. Place the ring handle near one end of the curtain rod.

2. Ask a friend to see if he can move the ring handle across the rod without the washer and rod touching each other. Tell him to begin when you give the signal, "go." Also tell him to stop when you say "halt."

3. When you give the signal, also press the switch.

4. Each time your friend makes contact between the washer and the rod, the bell tattles by ringing. When this happens say "halt." Release the switch to break the circuit. This stops the bell from ringing.

5. Again at your signal "go" have your friend continue to try to reach the other end of the rod without ringing the bell.

6. The object of the test is to see how few times your friend rings the bell in moving the ring handle across the rod. If he can do this without ringing the bell, he has "nerves of steel."

7. Keep score on everyone that you test. Remember the lowest score is the winner— a zero is a perfect score.

Would you like to know if someone comes into your club house uninvited? If this happens to you and your club members, put a stop to it once and for all. All you need are easy-to-make burglar alarms connected to your doors and windows. Anyone opening a door or raising a window, automatically starts an electric bell ringing. Of course, you can come in and out of the doors all day long without ringing the bell. You know its secret. You can make it sound an alarm, or you can make it keep silent. You will see how to do this as you work on the project.

Burglar alarm

What you need:

mercury switch

6 volt dry cell battery

electric bell (from hardware store or make one as described on page 101.)

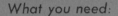

25' or more of bell wire

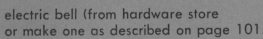

wood ¾" thick 1½" x 6"

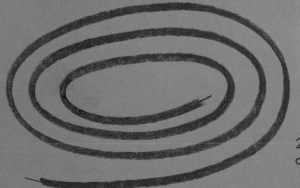

¼" x 4" dowel pin

(A 4" piece of pencil makes a good substitute.)

Your burglar alarm has many other uses, too. You may want to fasten one to each door in your home. CAUTION: If you decide to do this, get the help of your father. A nail or screw fastened in the wrong place might damage the woodwork or plaster. You may also want to know when someone comes in the front gate. If so, a burglar alarm lets you know quickly. It can even be set so that if someone drives your family automobile out of the driveway, you know about it before the car moves more than a few inches.

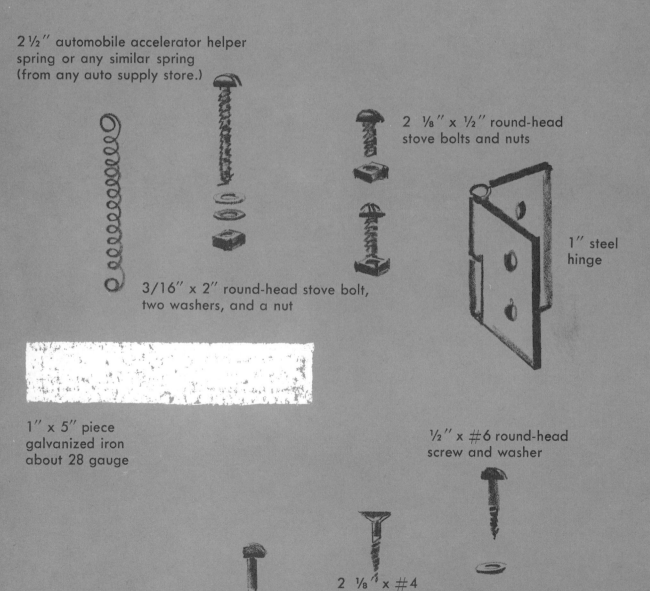

2 ½" automobile accelerator helper spring or any similar spring (from any auto supply store.)

2 ⅛" x ½" round-head stove bolts and nuts

1" steel hinge

3/16" x 2" round-head stove bolt, two washers, and a nut

1" x 5" piece galvanized iron about 28 gauge

½" x #6 round-head screw and washer

2 ⅛" x #4 flat head screws

(from any hardware store.)

1 ¼" x #6 round-head screw

Fasten the hinge to the edge of the wood block with the 2 ⅛″ x #4 flat-head screws.

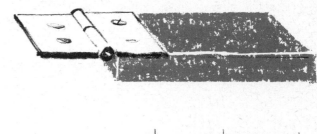

Using a 3/16″ bit, drill a hole in the center and 3″ from the hinged end of the wood block. You have just made the bracket.

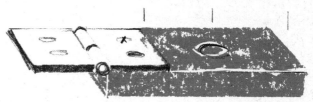

Place a washer on the 3/16″ x 2″ round-head stove bolt. Then run the bolt through the hole in the wood block. Be sure the shank of the bolt and the hinge face each other. Place a second washer on the bolt. Then tighten the nut. This is called the contact bolt.

Drill 2 ⅛″ holes near the edge of the galvanized iron strip. They must be in line with the two holes in the hinge. Round off the corners. Using a file, remove any burrs that might be left on the edges.

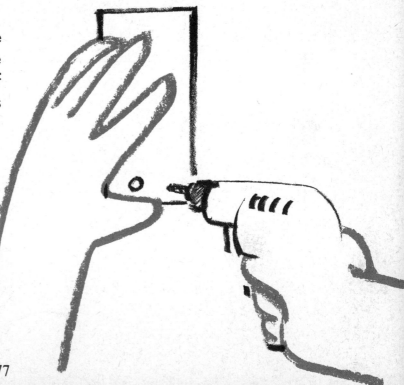

Using the 2 ⅛″ x ½″ round-head bolts and nuts, fasten the piece of galvanized iron to the hinge.

Using a pair of pliers, bend the piece of galvanized iron as shown.

Drill a ⅛″ hole in the galvanized piece of iron near the edge and ⅝″ from the hinged end. This completes the trigger.

Fasten one end of the spring in the trigger hole. Using the ½″ x #6 screw and washer, fasten the other end of the spring to the wood block edge, opposite the contact bolt. This screw also serves later on as a terminal for making one of the electrical connections.

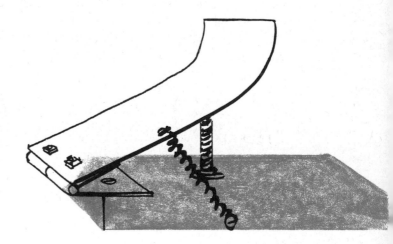

Drill a 3/16″ hole through the middle of the wide side of the bracket ½″ from the end opposite the hinge. This is the bracket mounting hole.

The burglar alarm you just made works for a 2½″ wide door casing. If your door casing is a different width, you may need to alter the bracket and trigger dimensions accordingly.

Using the 1¼″ x #6 round-head wood screw, fasten the burglar alarm to the top of the inside door casing.

Locate the battery, bell, and mercury switch in a convenient place. Next using bell wire, connect them together in series.

Using bell wire, connect the free wire from the switch to the screw terminal on the bracket. Also connect the free terminal on the bell to the 3/16″ x 1¼″ stove bolt, which also acts as a terminal.

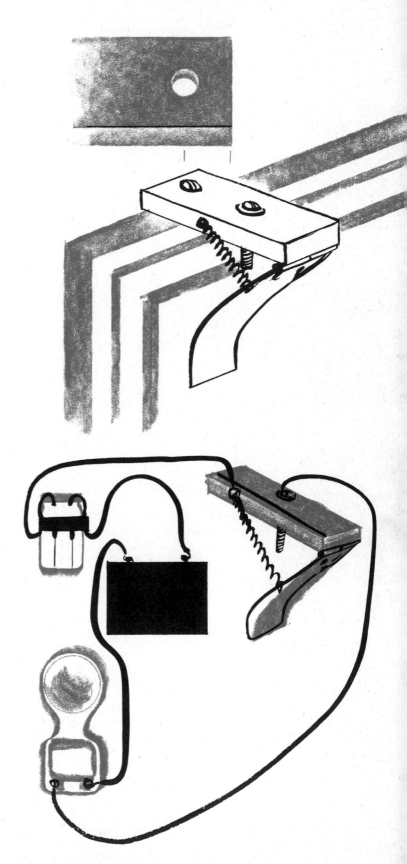

If the mercury switch is not tilted, the bell should ring. If it does not, re-check your connections. Be sure they are clean and tight as well as wired correctly.

To set the burglar alarm, place the dowel pin between the closed door and the trigger. Be sure the switch is in an upright position.

When the door opens, the dowel pin falls to the floor. The trigger slides over the door. Then the spring pulls the trigger to the contact bolt. This completes the circuit and the alarm bell rings until the circuit is open again. This can be done either by resetting the trigger with the dowel pin or by tilting the mercury switch. CAUTION: During the day, tilt the switch. This makes it possible to use the door without the alarm bell ringing.

Your burglar alarm has many uses. In fact, it can be used to tell you when an uninvited person is trespassing or trying to take something. With a slight change in bracket style, it can be attached to a window. Then if someone raises the window, the alarm sounds.

Look at the picture. See how it can guard your family automobile. As the thief moves the car, the trigger hits the contact bolt. With the circuit closed, the alarm rings. Here the dowel pin is not used to set the alarm. Notice that the circuit is opened by placing part of the tire between the contact bolt and the trigger.

You can use several alarm systems with the same battery and bell. Simply connect all of the alarms in parallel.

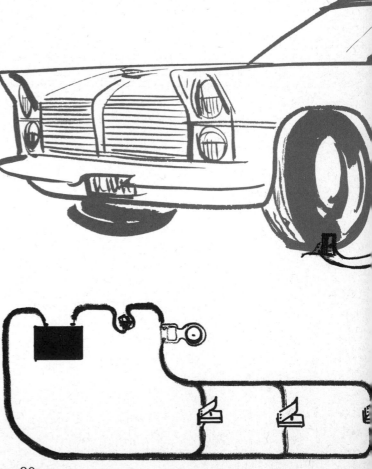

Would you or your parents like to know if the temperature suddenly goes too high or too low? And would it be helpful if you could be warned about this change anytime, day or night?

If you or any member of your family raise flowers or other crops requiring warm weather, such information might be helpful. Many crops can be protected from sudden cold if low temperature drops are known in time.

Temperature alarm

What you need:

baseboard ¾" thick
4" x 5"

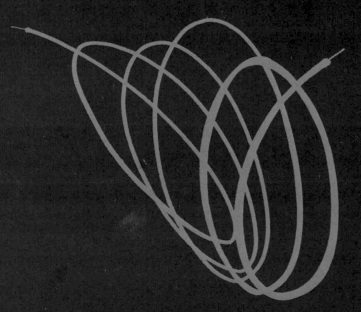

25' bell wire

If you have a stove or furnace that might overheat, it would be helpful to know it before the fire spread and got out of control. Here your temperature alarm would serve as a fire alarm. You might even discover the overheated system long before a fire started.

The temperature alarm is a wonderful instrument. It rings when a temperature you want to know about is reached. All you do is set it and forget it.

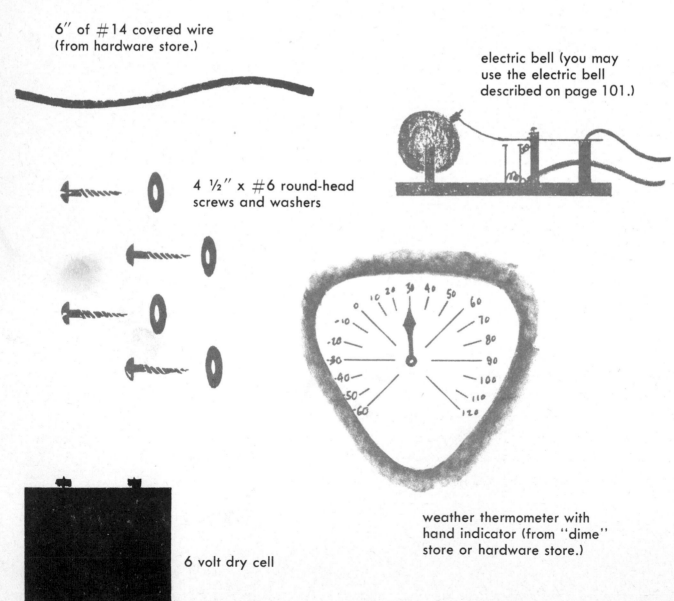

6" of #14 covered wire (from hardware store.)

electric bell (you may use the electric bell described on page 101.)

4 ½" x #6 round-head screws and washers

weather thermometer with hand indicator (from "dime" store or hardware store.)

6 volt dry cell

Remove the face cover of the thermometer. If it is glass and cannot be removed easily, break it. CAUTION: Take care not to be cut. If you must break the glass, protect your eyes from flying glass.

Using a sharp knife, carefully scrape the enamel or paint off the edges of the indicator hand.

If the face cover is plastic, drill a ⅛″ hole in it with a steel bit in line with the indicator and at the temperature markings desired. Here 32°, 90°, and 120°, are the temperatures wanted.

Using a ½″ x #6 screw and washer, fasten the thermometer mount to the ¾″ x 4″ x 5″ board. If no mount is included, fasten by drilling a hole through the thermometer case. CAUTION: Be sure not to drill into the temperature coil. This is usually found directly under the indicator hand.

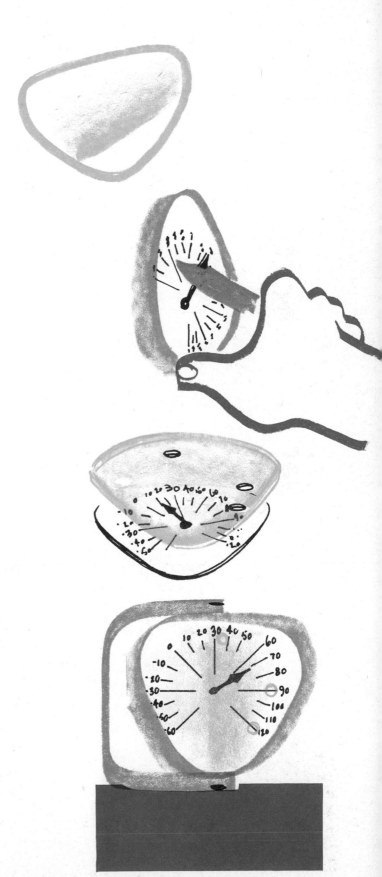

Fasten two ½″ x #6 screws and washers to the board in front of the thermometer. These serve as wire connecting terminals.

Scrape off enamel or paint on the metal case about as large as one of the washers.

Using a ⅛″ bit, drill a hole through the scraped part of the metal case. Now fasten a ½″ x #6 screw and washer through the hole into the board. This is a terminal for fastening a piece of bell wire as a connection to the indicator hand. If your thermometer case is made of plastic, you will need to fasten a piece of bell wire directly to metal that is connected to the indicator hand.

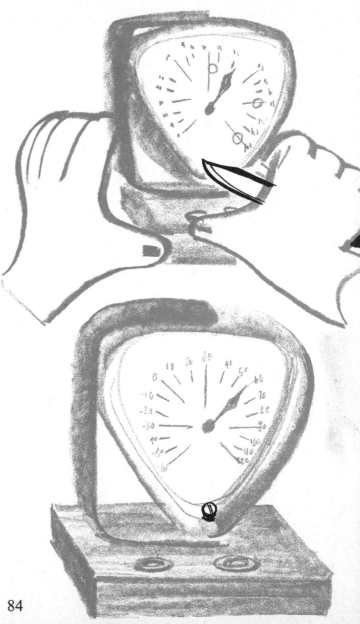

Connect a short piece of bell wire to the two screw terminals as shown.

Scrape about an inch of insulation off each end of the piece of #14 covered wire. Fasten one end to the third screw terminal as shown. Place the other end to the desired reading on the thermometer. In this case, 90° is the reading chosen. Be sure the reading is a little higher than the indicator hand shows.

Using pieces of bell wire, connect the 6 volt dry cell battery and electric bell in series to the two screw terminals fastened in the wood base.

Demonstrate the alarm system by holding a lighted 100 watt electric light bulb directly behind the indicator hand. Shortly the hand should move.

When the metal coil in the thermometer expands or contracts, the indicator hand moves. When it touches the #14 wire at the set reading, a complete circuit is formed. This sets off the electric bell. So whether it is day or night, you can be warned when a set temperature is reached.

To know when a set temperature is reached outside, simply place the thermometer out of doors. Run the bell wires to the batteries and electric bell inside the house. The warning bell will tell you if the temperature drops to an unsafe low.

If the stove or furnace might overheat, set the thermometer at about 110°. Place it near the heating system. Run the bell wires to the batteries and electric bell located in the bedroom. If overheating takes place, you will be warned long before the temperature is hot enough to set the house on fire.

Have you ever watched the electric-meter man read your meter and wished you knew what he was doing? After today you will know, and you can check on his readings.

An electric meter is a machine used to measure the electric power used. The unit of measure is based on the *watt*. A watt is the power carried by a current of one ampere flowing under an electrical pressure of one volt. One thousand watts make a *kilowatt*.

Electric companies charge a set price per kilowatt hour (KWH) used. A *kilowatt hour* is a unit of work that is done in one hour at a steady rate of one kilowatt. Some companies charge 5¢ per kilowatt hour. Other companies charge different prices. Usually cheaper rates are given people using large amounts of electricity. Electric companies call this a "special rate." Sometimes there is a "special rate" given for a meter connected to an electric range, dryer, or some other electric appliance.

How to read an electric meter

What you need:

an electric meter
to observe

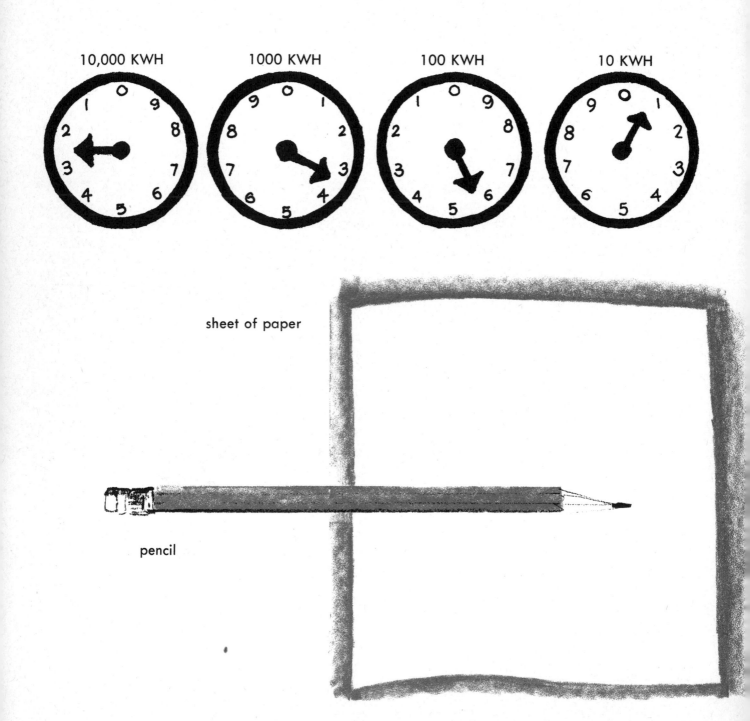

10,000 KWH   1000 KWH   100 KWH   10 KWH

sheet of paper

pencil

The secret of reading it is very simple, once you know how. An electric meter is read from the left dial to the right dial. When the hand on any dial points to the space between two numbers, the smallest number must be read.

Suppose your electric meter looks like the one pictured. Let's see the number of kilowatt hours used since the dials were set at zero.

Reading from left to right we find the meter shows the KWH at 4751.

Suppose a month later your meter looks like this:

Again reading from left to right, we find the meter shows the KWH at 4973.

    4973   Month later reading
  −4751   First reading
     222   KWH of electricity used
              during the month.

Suppose the rate is 5¢ per KWH.

    222
  x .05
 $11.10   cost of KWH of electricity used.

Now find out from your electric company the rate charged for your particular meter. Does it become lower the more KWH you use? You must have this information in order to figure your electric bill correctly.

Read your electric meter today and record the results in KWH. Read it again a month from now. Using your local rate, figure the cost of electricity used for the month. Review the example above to be sure you have not made a mistake.

Perhaps you have watched huge electric cranes picking up large pieces of iron and steel? Perhaps you have also found it interesting to see how easily great quantities of metal can be moved from place to place.

This project will show you exactly how an electric crane operates. In fact, you can make a miniature crane by fastening the horseshoe electromagnet to a toy crane.

Horseshoe electromagnet

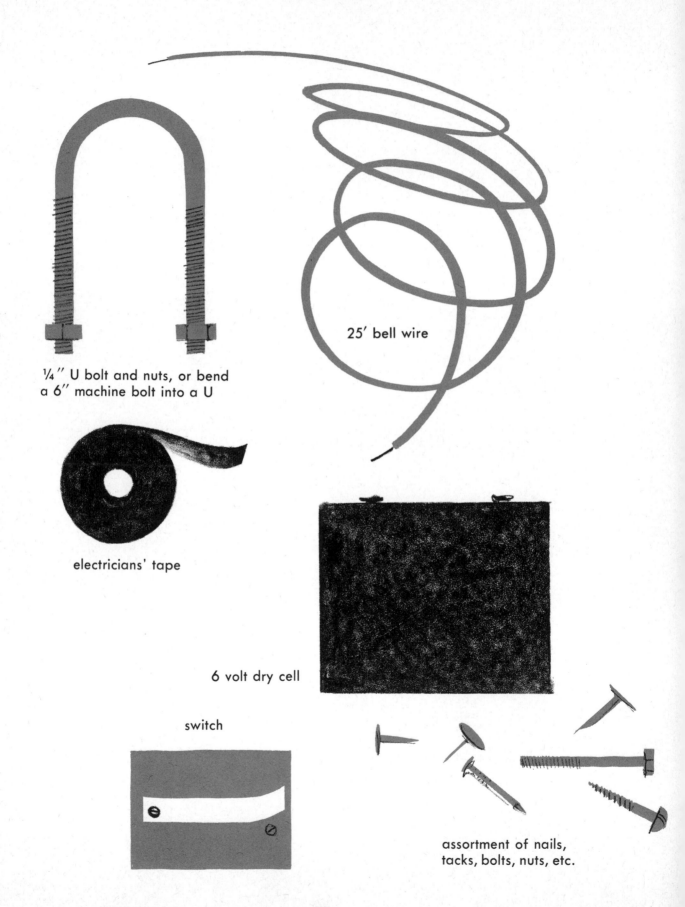

¼″ U bolt and nuts, or bend
a 6″ machine bolt into a U

25′ bell wire

electricians' tape

6 volt dry cell

switch

assortment of nails,
tacks, bolts, nuts, etc.

Begin at the bottom by winding a coil of five layers of bell wire in the same direction around one arm of the U bolt. Be sure the curved part of the bolt is free of wire. Then carry the wire across the top to the other bolt arm. Now wind the same number of turns but in the opposite direction. Leave about two feet of wire sticking out from the coils for making connections. CAUTION: For a horseshoe electromagnet to work, wire must be wound *clockwise* around one arm and *counterclockwise* around the other. This gives the magnet a North and a South pole. If both arms are wound in the same direction, both of the poles will be the same. If this happens, the magnet will not work.

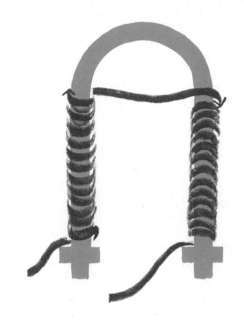

Wind a layer of electricians' tape around both coils to hold the wire in place.

Scrape the insulation from the ends of the magnet wires. Connect one wire to the switch and the other wire to one of the battery terminals. Using a piece of bell wire, connect the remaining switch terminal.

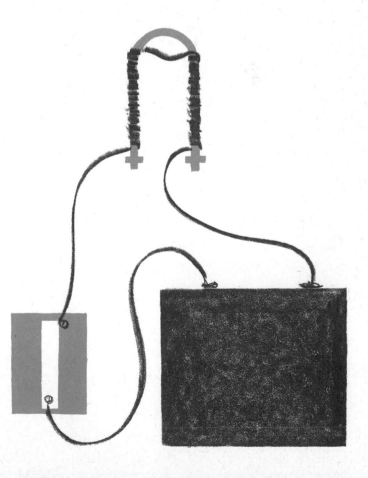

With one hand, bring the horseshoe electric magnet near the assortment of metal pieces. Use your free hand to close the switch. What happens? If you followed the directions carefully, the electromagnet picks up the metal pieces in much the same way as a permanent magnet does. When you release the switch, the circuit is open and the electromagnet can no longer hold the pieces of metal.

Here is an easy way to make an electric crane.

Using a piece of heavy string, hang the curved part of your electromagnet from the boom of a toy crane. You may want to fasten the switch with adhesive tape near the cab.

You have seen how electricity can be used to make a temporary magnet. Would you like to know how to strengthen *any* electromagnet? An electromagnet can be strengthened by either adding more turns of magnet wire to the iron core (U bolt in this project), or by adding more dry cell batteries connected in series. You may want to experiment by adding one or more 1½ volt dry cells and more magnet wire at the same time. You will have a stronger magnet by adding either one or both.

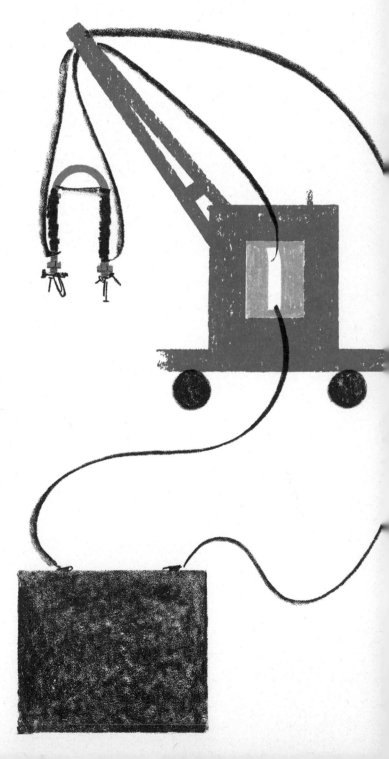

When you hear a telegraph set clicking, you wonder about it, don't you? And when you notice the clicks are different—some short, others long—you wonder some more.

Before you finish this project, you will learn why the telegraph clicks. You will also understand what the clicks mean. More than this, you may connect them so you can send messages from one room to another. Or you can even send messages between two houses.

Telegraph set

What you need:

(double the number of parts, except the
battery, if you wish to send messages to a friend)

6 volt dry cell

3 ½" x #4
round-head screws

5" x 2" piece of
galvanized iron
or heavy tin

wood ¾" thick
2" x 2"

25' bell wire

¾" x 3" galvanized
iron strip or
heavy tin

2 box-8 nails

2 1½" nails

plywood board 4" x 6"
(apple box crating
will also do.)

A telegraph set has two main parts—a *sounder* and a *sender*. Start by making the sounder.

Using the two 1½″ nails, fasten the ¾″ x 2″ x 2″ block of wood to the 4″ x 6″ plywood board as shown.

With tin snips, cut a T strip from the scrap piece of tin as shown. Remove rough edges and burrs with a file.

With a ½″ x #4 screw, fasten the T strip to the wood block.

With the T strip propped up out of the way, drive the two box-8 nails 1¾″ apart so that the heads will be 2″ above the plywood board.

Make the key by punching a hole in the middle and near one end of the ¾″ x 3″ galvanized iron strip. Then use one of the ½″ x #4 round-head screws to fasten it to the plywood board.

Now put a bend in the key, so the free end is about ½″ above the plywood board.

Fasten the remaining ½″ x #4 round-head screw to the plywood board underneath the free end of the key.

Scrape the insulation from one end of the bell wire. Connect it to the round-head screw under the key. Be sure to make a tight connection.

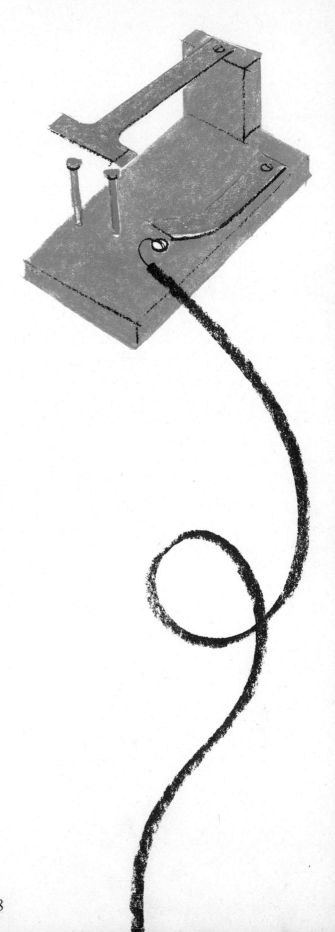

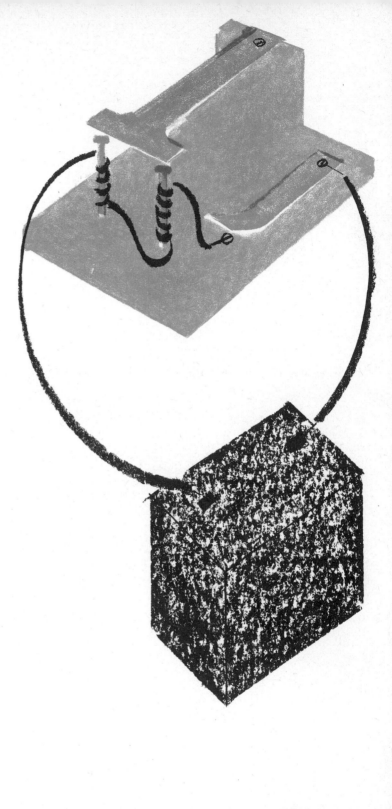

Now begin winding the bell wire in a clockwise direction from top to bottom of one nail. Then wind the wire around the second nail from bottom to top in a counter-clockwise (opposite) direction. Wind about 30 turns of wire on each nail. You will need to wind back and forth on each nail to wrap the 30 turns of bell wire in place. But remember this: No matter how many times you wind back and forth, the windings on the first nail should end at the bottom. The winding on the second nail should end on the top, near the head.

Cut the bell wire about a foot from the second nail. After removing the insulation from the end, connect it to one of the 6 volt dry cell terminals. Now connect the remaining dry cell terminal to the remaining terminal on the key. Be sure all connections are clean and tight.

Be sure the space between the T-shaped sounder strip and the nail heads is about the thickness of a table knife. If so, try out the set by pressing the key and then releasing it. You should hear a click from the sounder strip. You may have to adjust the space between the T strip and the nail heads several times to get a good click. Do this by slightly bending the metal.

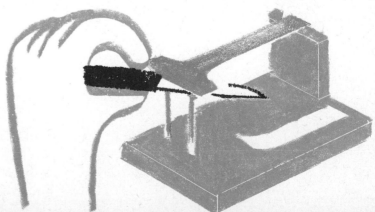

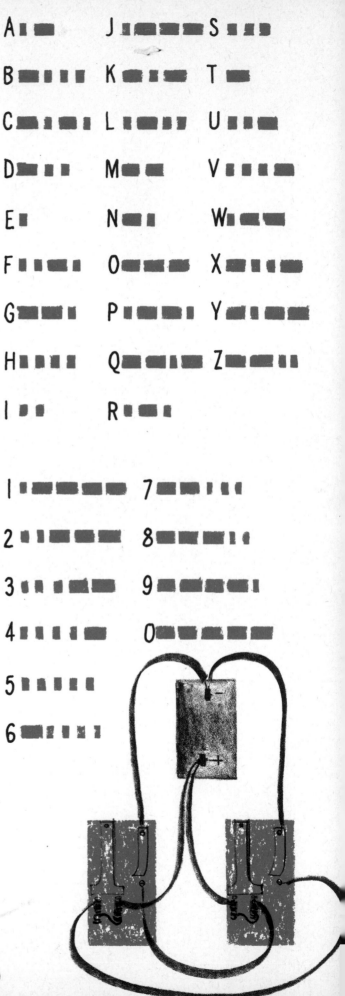

Here is the way your set works: When you press the key, you simply close the electric circuit. The two nails and the coil of wire act as an electromagnet. So when the key makes contact, the circuit closes and the electromagnet attracts the T-sounder strip. When the key is released, the circuit is open, releasing the power of the electromagnet. This causes the T-sounder strip to be released. The time between clicks depends on how long you keep the key down.

Morse Code is used by many telegraphers. A long space between clicks is called a *dash,* while a short space is called a *dot.* You may want to make up a code all of your own. Again you may want to learn to use the standard Morse Code. This is especially true if you want to make two telegraph sets. With this, it is possible to send and receive messages. To do this, all you need do is to make a second set and connect them as shown.

Did you know that without electromagnets there would be no electric bells? Yes, an electromagnet is one of the important parts of any electric bell. Yet, if you want to have one, you need not buy one. You can make it quickly and easily, and have a lot of fun doing it.

Electric bell

What you need:

6 volt dry cell

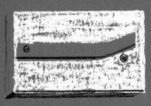

switch

2 ½″ x #6 round-head screws and washers

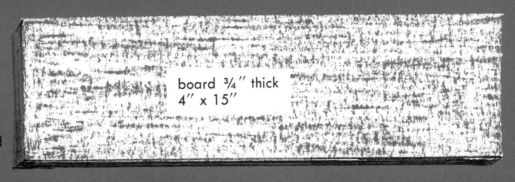

board ¾″ thick
4″ x 15″

2 ½″ x #6 flat-head screws

wood ¾″ thick
3″ x 3 ¾″

You will find many other uses for your electric bell. You can use it as part of your Nerve Machine as described on page 71. You can proudly show your friends how the vibrator, the hammer, the gong, and the electromagnet all work together to make the bell ring. You will know how, because you put the parts together.

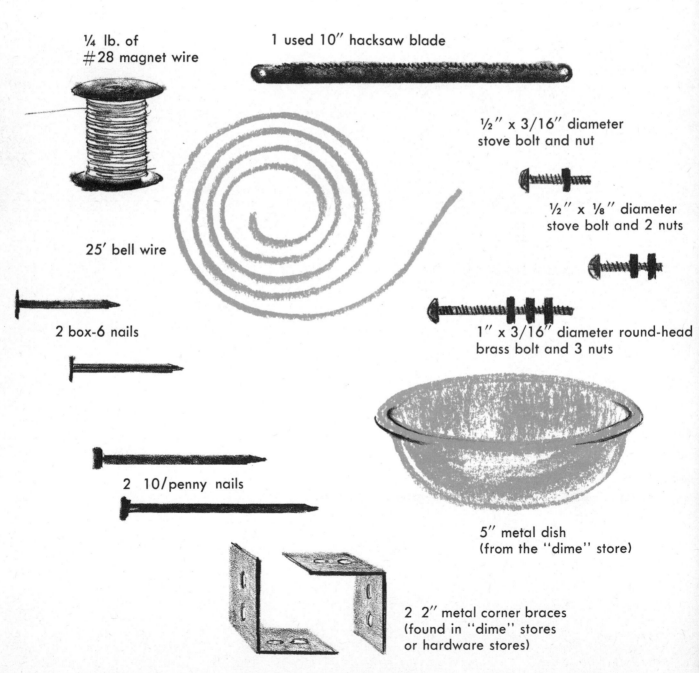

¼ lb. of
#28 magnet wire

1 used 10" hacksaw blade

½" x 3/16" diameter
stove bolt and nut

½" x ⅛" diameter
stove bolt and 2 nuts

25' bell wire

2 box-6 nails

1" x 3/16" diameter round-head
brass bolt and 3 nuts

2 10/penny nails

5" metal dish
(from the "dime" store)

2 2" metal corner braces
(found in "dime" stores
or hardware stores)

Using a hammer, drive the two box-6 nails through the baseboard into the wood block. Be sure it is placed even with the baseboard on one side and 1½″ from the end as shown.

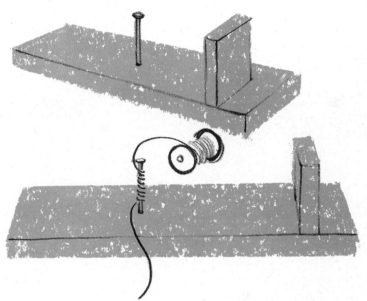

Drive one of the 10/penny nails almost through the middle of the baseboard and 6½″ from the end opposite the wood block.

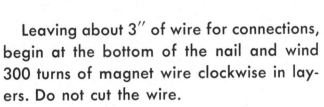

Leaving about 3″ of wire for connections, begin at the bottom of the nail and wind 300 turns of magnet wire clockwise in layers. Do not cut the wire.

Drive the second 10/penny nail into the baseboard the same as before with this difference. Place it 1½″ closer to the wood block.

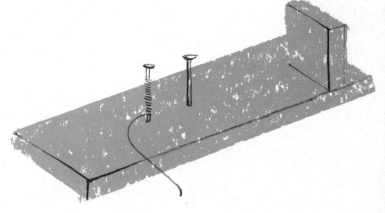

Bring the magnet wire over to the bottom of the second nail. Now wind 300 turns of magnet wire clockwise in layers. Be sure to end near the top of the nail. Again, leave about 3″ of wire sticking out for connections. Wrap two turns of plastic tape around the top of the nail to keep the coil of wire from unwinding. Your electromagnet is now complete.

Using a hammer, flatten out the two corner braces. This makes them flat pieces of strip iron.

Using a vise and a hammer, bend a ½″ lip at right angles (L) on one end of one of the pieces.

Using one of the ½″ x #6 flat-head screws, fasten the strap iron 2″ from the end of the baseboard and near the edge as shown. This is the gong bracket.

104

Using a 3/16″ metal bit, drill a hole about ⅛″ off center in the metal dish. This is the gong.

Fasten the gong to the top hole in the gong bracket with the ½″ x ⅛″ stove bolt and two nuts. Be sure a nut is on either side of the gong.

Using a ¼″ steel bit, open the hole in one end of the hacksaw blade. Now run the ½″ x 3/16″ stove bolt through the hole and fasten in place with the nut. This makes up the vibrator and hammer.

With a ½″ x #6 round-head screw, fasten the other end of the vibrator to the wood block. Be sure the vibrator is lined up exactly over the heads of the two armature nails. Now bend it so the hammer almost touches the gong.

With a vise and hammer, bend ½"
lips at right angles (L) on each end on
opposite sides of the second piece of
strap iron as shown. A hole should fall
in the middle of each lip. This is the
contact point support.

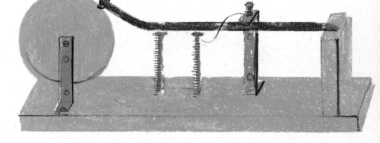

Fasten the contact point support to
the base with a ½" x #6 flat-head
screw at a point about 3½" from the
wood block. Be sure the hole in the
support lip is directly over the vibrator.

Use the 1" x 3/16" bolt and 2 nuts
for a contact point as shown. The third
nut is used later for making a tight
connection from the electromagnet
wire. Now screw the contact point
down so the vibrator will stand out
about ⅛" from the magnet nail heads.

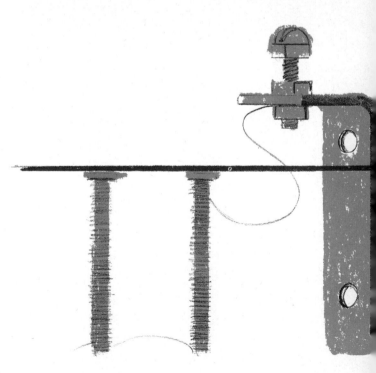

The remaining ½" x #6 round-
head screw and washer serve as a
terminal. Fasten the screw over the
washer part way down near the edge
of the baseboard and opposite the
contact point support.

Using bell wire, connect the 6 volt dry cell battery and switch. Then connect a lead wire about 16″ long to the remaining battery terminal and another to the remaining switch terminal.

Scrape the insulation from the ends of the armature magnet wire and the bell wire leads. Fasten the magnet wire next to the base (A) and the end of the switch wire lead (B) to the screw terminal (C). Fasten the second armature wire (D) next to the head of the contact point bolt (E). Use the third 3/16″ nut for making a tight connection between the electromagnet wire and the head of the contact bolt. You should have two nuts above the contact point support and one nut below it. Fasten the end of the battery lead wire (F) to the screw (G) holding the vibrator.

Press the switch. Does the bell ring? If it does not ring or rings a little bit, do not quit. Some adjustments are usually needed before the bell rings at its best. If you can answer "yes" to these questions, your bell should work perfectly.

1. Are the parts mounted as given in the directions?

2. Are the coils of magnet wire wound in the right direction?

3. Does the vibrator make good contact against the contact point. If not, be sure to sand the contact point and the place of contact on the vibrator.

4. Is the vibrator close to the magnet nail heads, but not touching? Always screw

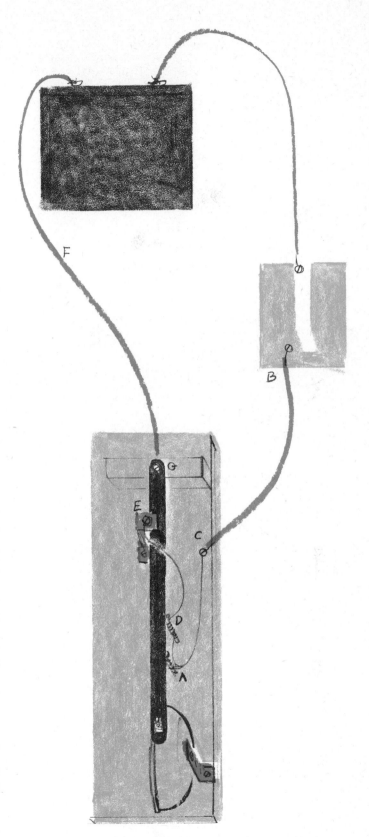

the contact bolt up and down until the bell sounds its best.

5. Is the hammer at the end of the vibrator slightly away from the gong? Here you may need to bend the vibrator until the hammer makes the best contact against the gong when the bell rings. Fine adjustments between the hammer and gong can be made by turning the gong slightly. Remember the hole was drilled off center. So turning the gong causes it to either come closer or go farther away from the hammer.

6. Are all connections clean and tight? Do not overlook the vibrator contact screw. Sometimes hacksaw blades leave some paint around the holes. If so with yours, sand and clean or a good connection cannot be made.

This is why the bell works. When you press the switch, the circuit is closed. The electric current flows from the battery into the electromagnet. This causes the electromagnet to attract or pull the vibrator away from the contact point, and the hammer hits the gong. At the instant the vibrator is pulled away from the contact point, the circuit is broken (open). Since the vibrator acts as a spring, it quickly returns to the contact point. For with the circuit open, the magnet loses its power. Of course just as soon as con-

tact is again made between the vibrator and contact point, the magnet again attracts the vibrator. And once again the cycle is repeated. Since this is done faster than "a cat can wink his eye," the hammer strikes the gong over and over as long as the switch is closed.

In short, your electric bell works on the principle of quickly making and breaking an electric circuit.

Would you like to have a real telephone set so you can talk to someone in another room? Or perhaps you would like to string up a telephone line between two club houses. You can do this and more if you make the two microphones described here and the two receivers described in the next project.

Telephone carbon microphone

What you need:
(for two carbon microphones)

1″ carbon rod from middle of old 1 ½ volt dry cell
(Some dry cells are not made with a simple carbon rod. Rather, they contain five
small batteries, each with a 5/16″ carbon rod.
These can supply you with carbon rods next on the list.)

25′ bell wire

2 5/16″ x 2″ carbon rods
(Old flashlight battery or from the type of dry cell battery described before.)

Since the telephone sets and battery are portable, they also can be used for communications between squad leaders of make-believe army patrols.

4 ½″ x 3″ strips of tin
(May be cut from an empty tin can.)

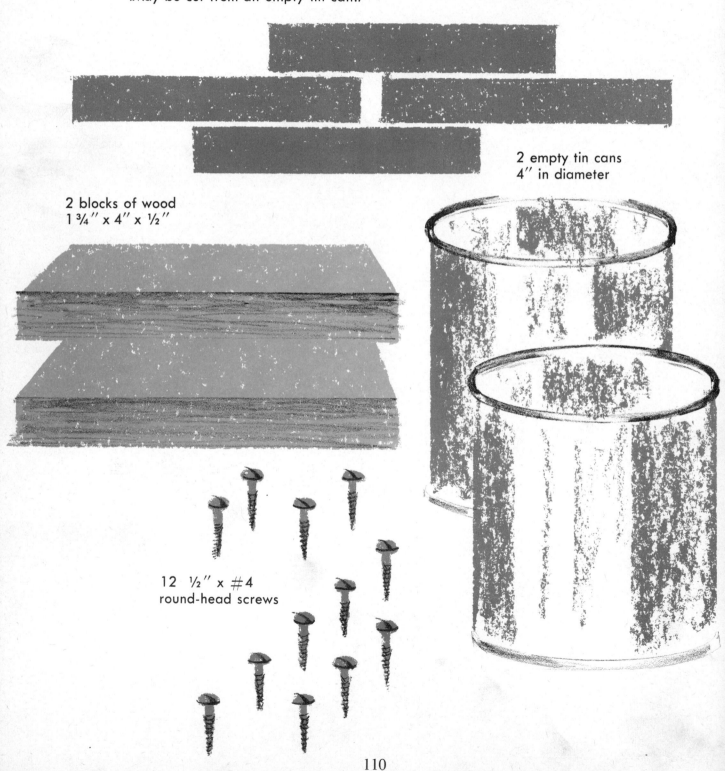

2 empty tin cans
4″ in diameter

2 blocks of wood
1 ¾″ x 4″ x ½″

12 ½″ x #4
round-head screws

Using a hacksaw, cut four one-inch pieces from the large carbon rod.

Make a cone-shaped hole in the center of each end. The best way to do this is with a carpenter's countersink and brace. If you do not have these tools, make the holes with a pocket knife or with a sharpened file point.

Using a pencil sharpener, point the ends of the two 5/16″ x 2″ carbon rods. If you do not have a pencil sharpener, point the ends with a file.

The next step is the cutting of the wood blocks. Before cutting them, use a pencil to mark the correct curve taken from the end of one of the tin cans.

Now cut the blocks of wood so that they will fit tightly in the open ends of the cans. Be sure the cans have one end completely removed, and the openings are free from burrs.

Using a hammer and a box-8 nail, punch holes in the ends of the tin strips.

Be sure the corners are rounded on the tin strips and that no burrs are left. Use a file or a piece of coarse emery paper for this job.

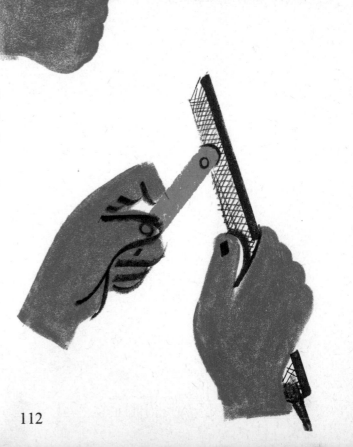

Using 8 of the ½″ x #4 round-head screws and tin strips, mount the large carbon pieces.

Next fit the sharpened carbon rods in place in the cone-shaped holes. These rods should never fit tight.

make two microphones

Now cut 4 pieces of bell wire about 14″ long. Scrape the insulation from each end. These are the connection wires. Fasten one end of each wire as shown. CAUTION: Be sure the screws are tight and that the sharpened carbon rods fit loosely and are free to move. They must be free to vibrate later when sound waves strike them.

Using a ¼″ metal bit, drill a hole in the center of the ends of each can.

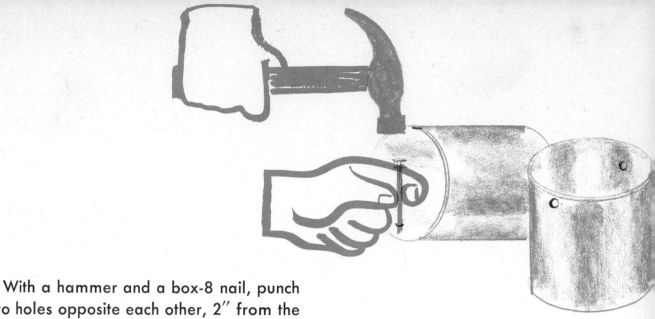

With a hammer and a box-8 nail, punch two holes opposite each other, 2″ from the open end of each can.

Using 2 ½″ #4 round-head screws for each can, mount the wood block containing the carbon pieces as shown. Be sure the connecting wires are placed through the holes in the closed ends of the cans.

You are now ready to make the two receivers as explained in the next project. When this is done, you will be ready to put your own telephone line to work.

Telephone receiver

What you need:
(for two telephone receivers and completing the telephone line)

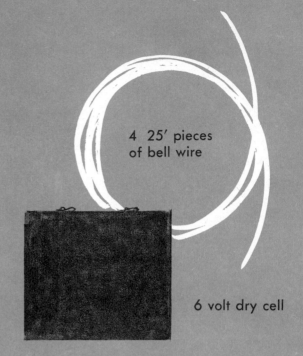

4 25′ pieces of bell wire

6 volt dry cell

switch

½ lb. of #28 magnet wire

acetic acid vinegar

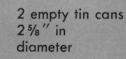

2 empty tin cans 2⅝″ in diameter

2 blocks of wood
¾″ x 2⅝″
½″ thick

small can of enamel

1″ paint brush

2 box-8 nails

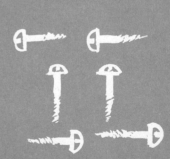

8 ½″ x #4 round-head screws

Begin by cutting the blocks of wood to fit the openings of the tin cans. Do this in the same way as in the last project. Use a pencil to mark the correct curve taken from the end of one of the tin cans. Be sure the cans have one end completely removed and the openings are free from burrs.

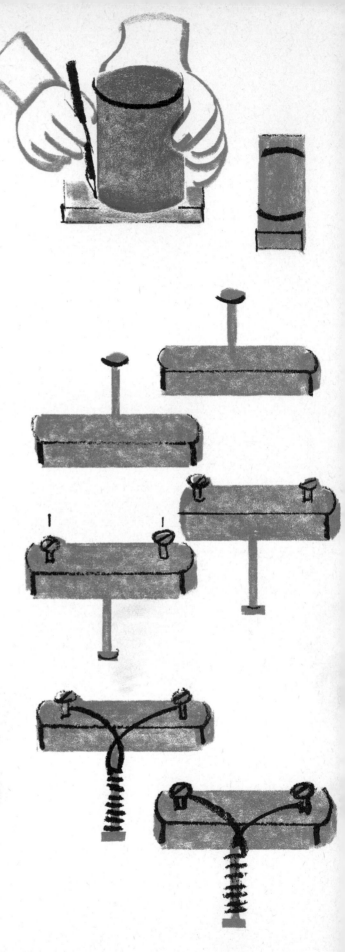

Using a hammer drive the box-8 nails about ¼" in the middle of the wide edge of the wood blocks.

Screw 2 ½" x #4 round-head screws, about 1 ¼" apart, on the opposite side of each wood block.

Wind 800 turns of the magnet wire in one direction around each of the box-8 nails. Leave about 3" of wire sticking out from each end.

Scrape the insulation from the ends of the wires and fasten each to one of the screws. You have just made the receivers' electromagnets.

Cut 4 pieces of bell wire about 14″ long for making the connecting wires. Scrape off the insulation from each end. Then fasten one end of each wire as shown. Now fasten the screws tight so good connections are made between the ends of magnet wire and bell wire ends.

Using a ¼″ metal bit, drill a hole in the side of the cans about 1″ from the closed ends.

With a hammer and a box-8 nail, punch two holes, opposite each other, ¼″ from the open end of each can.

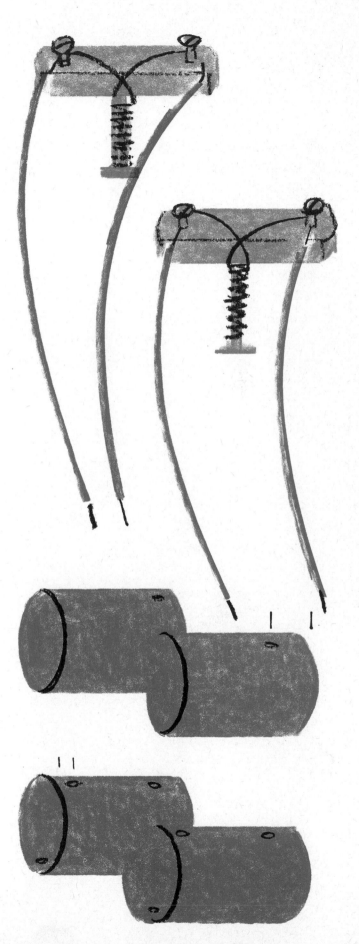

Put the electromagnets (coil first) into the cans until the nail heads touch the can bottoms. Be sure the connecting wires are placed through the holes in the sides of the cans. Next press down slightly on the center of the bottom of the cans to force the nail heads back just a little. Since the can bottoms must vibrate against the nail heads, the space between them must be 1/16 of an inch. CAUTION: If the blocks of wood fit tightly, press the sides of the cans slightly together until the blocks are placed in position.

Now check your receivers one at a time. Connect a receiver connecting wire to the terminal of the dry cell battery. Now touch the free end of the other receiver connecting wire to the remaining battery terminal. You should hear a scratching or a popping noise.

Using 2 ½″ #4 round-head screws for each can, fasten the electromagnet firmly in place as shown. Be sure the wood block does not move.

Now make two complete telephone units by fastening a microphone and receiver together with clothes-hanger wire or other soft iron wire.

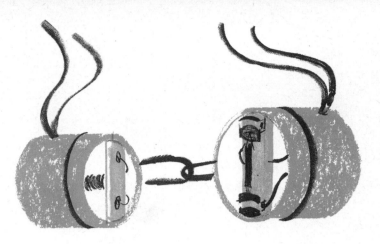

Paint the outside of the microphone and receiver two coats of paint of your own choice. Before applying paint, do these two things:

1. Remove labels and dirt from outside of cans.

2. Prepare tin surfaces for painting by cleaning outside of cans with vinegar made from acetic acid. Rinse with clear water. When dry, apply paint.

When paint has dried, use bell wire to connect the two microphones, two receivers, switch, and dry cell battery in series.

Station yourself at the telephone set with the switch. Have a friend use the set in the next room. Close the circuit by pressing the switch. Put your mouth close to the opening in the microphone can and talk. Your friend should be able to hear you in his receiver.

If you have followed the directions carefully, your telephone line should be trouble free. If not, make these checks:

1. Are the carbon rods loose and free to move in the microphones?

2. Is each connection clean and tight?

3. Did you close the switch when either you or your friend were talking?

4. Do you really have a closed circuit when the switch is closed? Remember that a single break in any of the wiring, including the electromagnet coils, will prevent the telephone sets from working.

5. Is your battery alive? You may want to check it with your electric current detector or a six-volt automobile light bulb.

If you can answer "yes" to the five questions above, your telephone sets should give you a lot of pleasure and fun.

You have seen how dry and wet cells generate electric currents by chemical reaction. You know, too, that these cells have a short life. They must be replaced often.

Perhaps you know that the electricity coming into your home is generated by big machines called *generators*. This is a much simpler and less expensive method than using batteries. It makes the price of electricity small enough so we can use it to do much of our work.

Electric generator

What you need:

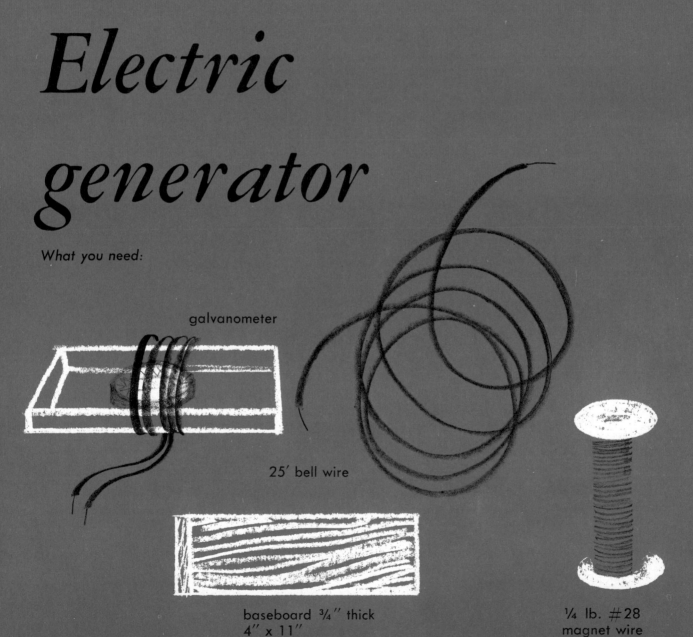

galvanometer

25′ bell wire

baseboard ¾″ thick
4″ x 11″

¼ lb. #28
magnet wire

horseshoe permanent magnet
(from a dime store)

In this project, you will learn the principle of generating electricity with an easy-to-make generator. You will also make a water wheel to furnish power for the generator. Both are interesting and fascinating. And you can also have a lot fun showing your friends how electricity is generated.

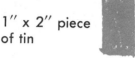

1″ x 2″ piece
of tin

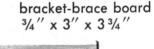

½″ x 8″ dowel
pin

bracket-brace board
¾″ x 3″ x 3¾″

2 support boards
¾″ x 3″ x 6″

bracket board
¾″ x 3″ x 5½″
(If your magnet size is
different than the one
given below, change size
of these boards to fit.)

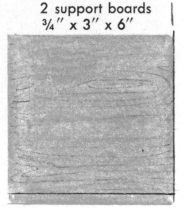

10 ½″ x #4
round-head screws

board ¾″ thick
6″ x 6″

2 washers for
½″ screws

2 ½″ washers

6 coffee jar or similar lids
about 2½″ in diameter

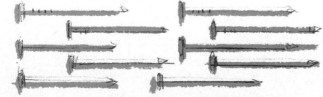

10 box-6 nails

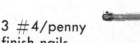

3 #4/penny
finish nails

Drill a 9/16″ hole in the middle and 1½″ from one end of each support board.

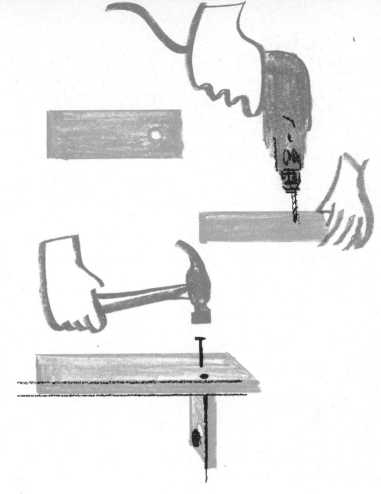

Using two box-6 nails, fasten one of the support boards 1″ from the end and ⅝″ from each side of the baseboard. Drive the nails through the baseboard into the end of the support board. Be sure the hole is near the end not fastened to the baseboard.

Nail the second support board to the baseboard. Do this exactly as before but space it 5″ from the first one.

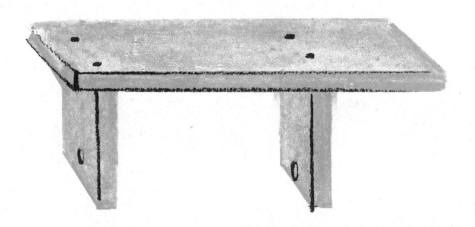

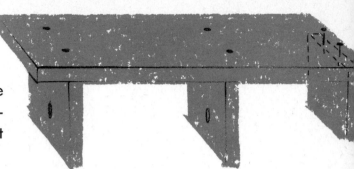

Now fasten with two box-6 nails the bracket-brace board at the end of the baseboard and in line with the two support boards.

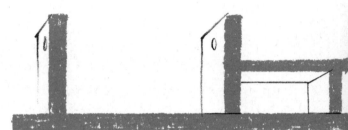

Fasten the bracket board to the bracket-brace board with two box-6 nails through the second support directly into the end of the bracket. Be sure the bracket is level with the baseboard.

Find the center of the six-inch-square board by making a pencil line from each corner to the opposite one.

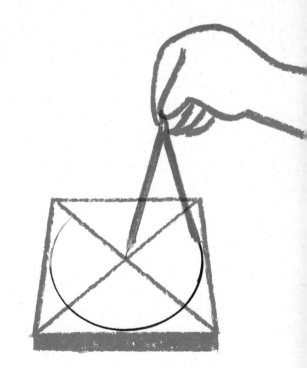

Place one leg of an artist's compass exactly on the point where the lines cross and make a 5″ circle.

Now drill a ½" hole where the lines cross.

Using a jig saw or key-hole saw, cut along the curved line to make a 5" wheel.

Using a pencil and tape measure, mark the outside of the wheel in six places the same distance apart. This is about 2¾".

Make a hole in the edge of each coffee can lid with a box-6 nail.

Using a ½" x #6 screw, fasten each lid directly over a pencil mark on the outside of the wheel as shown.

Using a hand saw, cut a notch in one end of the dowel pin ¼″ deeper than the width of your horseshoe. For the one shown in "things needed," ⅝″ is about right.

Slip the wooden wheel over the dowel pin so that it sticks out about as far on one side as the other.

Hold the wheel in place by driving a #4/penny finish nail at an angle through the side of the wheel and into the dowel pin.

Place a ½″ washer over the end of the uncut dowel pin and mount the wheel assembly in the support holes. Be sure that about the same amount of dowel pin sticks out on both sides. Also put the second ½″ washer in place as shown.

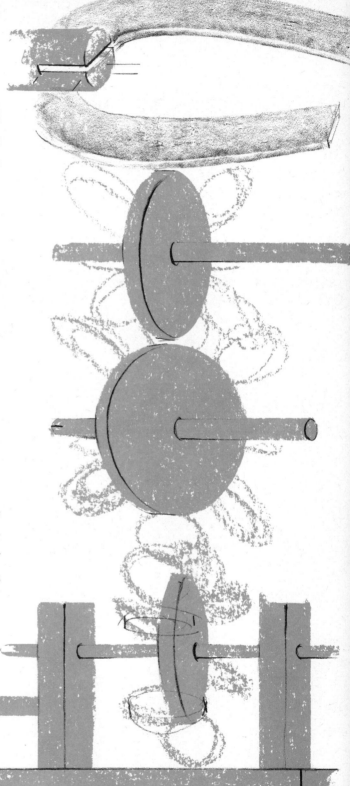

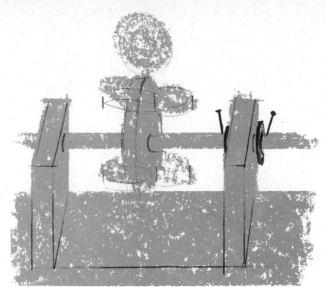

Drive two #4/penny finish nails through the dowel pin on the outside of each washer. Be sure there is enough space between the two washers so the wheel can spin freely. Your nails will drive easily if you will first drill a 1/16″ hole almost through the dowel pin at the nail locations. Be sure to test your wheel at this point. It should spin as freely as before the nails were driven. If it does not, your nails are driven too close together.

Make the coil by winding about 300 turns of #28 magnet wire in one direction around a paper cup. Leave about 4″ sticking out at each end for connections. Be sure the coil is large enough to easily clear the magnet.

Slip the coil from the cup and fasten it with plastic tape at about five points so it will not come apart.

Using a small nail, punch a hole in each end of the 1″ x 2″ piece of tin. Be sure to round the corners and to sand or file away any burrs.

Slide the magnet in place in the dowel pin notch. Be sure the magnet turns in an even circle when the wheel is turned.

Now place the coil of wire on the bracket board in such a way that the magnet points are on the inside.

Some adjustments on the horseshoe mount and the coil location may be in order. The magnet must turn inside the coil without touching it. Use the strip of tin and 2 ½″ x #4 screws to hold the coil in place.

Use a piece of bell wire about 6″ long to fasten the magnet to the dowel pin.

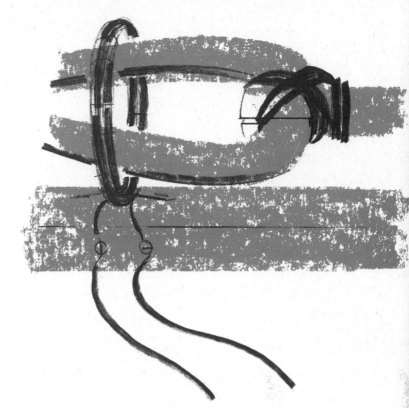

Scrape the insulation from the ends of the coil wires. Then use 2 ½″ x #4 screws and washers to connect the ends of the coil and lead wires from your compass galvanometer together. (Instructions for making a galvanometer are given on page 46.) Your generator is now complete.

(connect wires to galvanometer)

Place your generator so the cups on the wheel are directly underneath a water faucet. Then turn on the water. (It is less messy to do this in the yard. If a faucet is not handy, use a garden hose.)

As the water makes the magnet turn fast, notice the compass needle move. As you know, this proves electricity is being generated. The reason for this is easy to explain:

A coil of wire placed in a magnetic field, generates electricity. In a commercial generator, an electromagnet is used instead of a permanent magnet.

Your generator is excellent to use in demonstrating how electricity is generated. Commercial generators are not very different than the one you built. They are actually built on principles of increasing the rate of electricity produced. These principles are easy to understand and can be used to increase the rate of electricity generated by any generator:

1. Increase the number of turns of wire in the coils.

2. Increase the strength of the magnet.

3. Increase the speed with which the coils or magnets move, depending on the kind of generator being used.

galvanometer

Do you know exactly how many electric motors work for you and your family in your own home? You might be surprised at the number if you stopped long enough to think where they are.

Electric

motor

What you need:

25' bell wire

½" roll of electricians' plastic tape

¼ lb. of #28 magnet wire

4 box-8 nails

switch

1 #30/penny spike nail

4 #10/penny finish nails

6 volt dry cell

An electric motor helps dad shave, if he uses an electric razor. There is an electric motor in the refrigerator. There is one in mother's hair dryer. Another runs the vacuum cleaner. Still another runs the furnace blower or the water pump. Motors run washing machines, dryers, air conditioners, electric fans and electric clocks, and many other household gadgets.

In this project you learn how to make the parts of an electric motor. You learn what their names are and how to put them together so the motor runs.

wood 4¼" x 6"
¾" thick

2 ¼" x 1" strips
of copper

2 ⅜" x 3½" strips
of copper

⅛" x ⅝" x 6" piece of strap iron
(from junk yard or welding shop.)

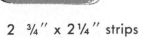

2 ¾" x 2¼" strips
cut from a tin can lid

8 ½" x #4 round-head screws

washer to fit tightly
on #30 spike nail

Begin by making the armature. Pick up two of the box-8 nails so that the point of one nail touches the head of the other.

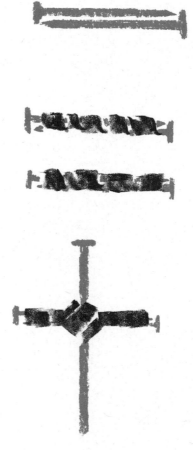

Wrap a layer of plastic tape around the two nails. Now do the same thing to the other two box-8 nails.

Make a cross with the #30/penny spike nail and the taped box-8 nails. Center the box-8 nails on a point 1¾" from the spike nail head. Hold cross in place with plastic tape as shown.

Start near the spike and wind about 600 turns of the #28 gauge wire in layers around the box-8 nails. Be sure to wind 300 turns of wire on each arm of the cross. Wrapping must be in the same direction (clockwise) on both sides of the spike. Leave about 3" of wire sticking out from each end. These are later used for making connections. Two turns of plastic tape around the last several wrappings of wire keeps the coil from unwinding.

#28 gauge insulated wire
300 turns on each arm
wrap clockwise on both arms

Your armature, one of the four important parts of the motor is complete. The commutator, brushes, and field magnet remain to be made.

Before making the commutator, wrap a layer of plastic tape on the spike for 1⅜″ below the armature coil.

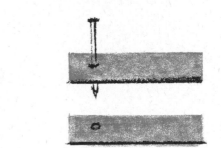

Using a small nail, make two small holes (1/16″) in the center near the end of each of the ¼″ x 1″ copper strip.

Using a pair of pliers, curve each one of the strips lengthwise to fit the spike.

Scrape the insulation from the ends of the armature connecting wires. Run each wire through a hole in one of the copper strips and fasten. Work carefully so the wires do not break. You may want to hold the wires in place with a drop of solder.

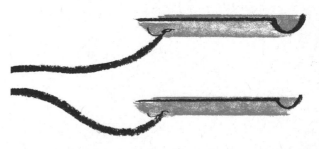

Mount the copper strips in place over the taped part of the spike. There should be ⅜″ distance between the armature and the near end of the strips. Also there should be about ⅛″ of space between the edges of the copper strips. Mount the strips in such a way that the two spaces are in line with the armature nail heads. Using short pieces of ¾″ plastic tape, hold the copper strips in place at top and bottom. Your commutator is now complete.

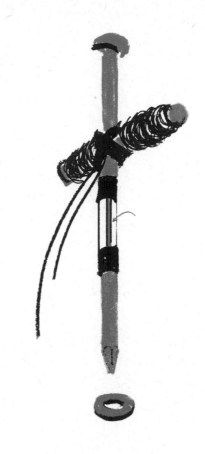

Drive the spike through the washer so that it is about ¾″ from the point.

Make the armature mount next. Using a pencil draw a light line lengthwise down the middle of the wood block.

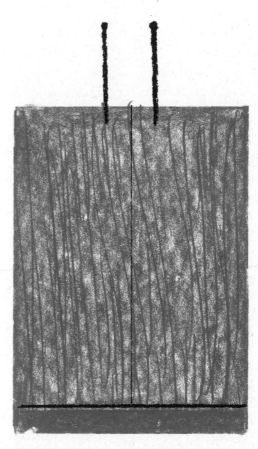

Drive two of the #10/penny finish nails almost through the board 3/16″ on either side of the line and ½″ from the edge.

Move down the line 3⅜″ and drive the other two #10/penny finish nails the same way as before.

Remove the insulation from two pieces of bell wire 4″ long. Then wind (toward the nail head) about three coils close together on one nail, beginning about 1½″ from the bottom of the board. Now carry the wire across to the nearest nail. Again wind about three coils toward the bottom of the nail. Do the same thing with the other pair of nails. The wires may need some adjustment later on. This completes your armature mount.

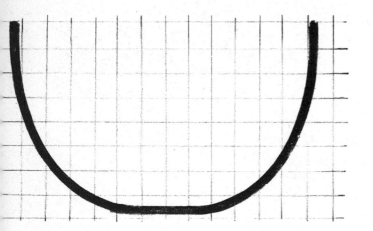

Using a pair of pliers and a vise, shape the strap iron flat on the bottom and curved on the sides so the armature can turn freely without touching. Use the full-size drawing as a pattern.

Beginning at one end of the flat part of the strap iron, wind 600 turns of the #28 gauge wire in layers. Leave about 3″ at each end for making connections. When finished, wind one layer of plastic tape around the coil. This completes the field.

Using a box-8 nail, punch a hole near the end of the two pieces of tin. These are used to mount the field.

Now put the armature in place as shown. It should fit loosely between the nails, resting on the bare bell wires. Be sure it is in the right direction.

Place the field directly under the armature coil. Turn the armature with your fingers. You should adjust the bell wire supports and the field so as the armature turns, it is close to the field but not touching it.

When you have the armature so it turns freely, mount the field in place with the tin strips and 4 ½″ x #4 round-head screws.

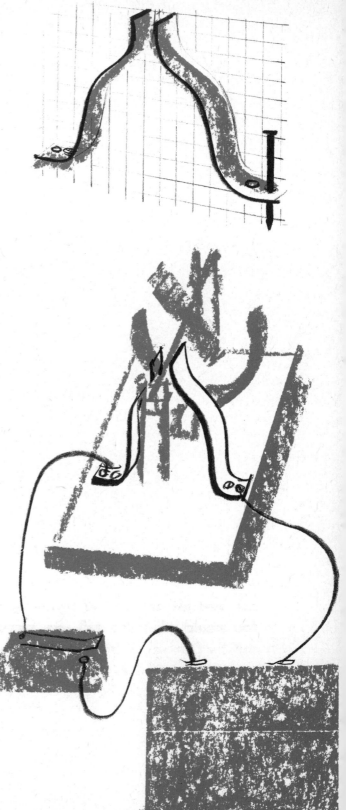

Form the brushes by shaping the two copper strips as shown in the full-size drawing.

Using a box-8 nail, punch two holes in each strip as shown.

With 4 ½″ x #4 round-head screws, mount the brushes in line with the middle of the commutator and about ¼″ from the edge of the wood block. Be sure the brushes touch the commutator very lightly.

Scrape the insulation from the field connecting wires. Then connect each one to the nearest brush terminal.

Using bell wire, connect the outside brush terminals, the switch, and the 6 volt dry cell battery in series.

Close the switch, and at the same time give the armature a turn. If your windings and connections are all as shown, your motor should run at a fast clip.

If your motor runs slowly, it may be helpful to tune up the brushes. Make sure they lie flat against the commutator. They should not be too tight or too loose. Bend the brushes until they make the best contact for a speedy motor. Be sure the armature turns freely and does not drag at any point on the field.

You may want to fasten a pulley from an erector set to the armature axle (spike). You may want to use a pulley made from an empty sewing spool.

The secret working parts of any electromagnet is found in its iron core and in its coil of wire. By now, you know they must be made and located correctly if the electromagnet is to work properly. The electromagnet projects you have built so far have the core, made of iron, on the inside. And the core is covered with a coil of wire.

Electric flag

Now you are going to learn how to make a different kind of electromagnet. This one is called a *solenoid*. Some people call it a "sucking coil." It is used in the electric flag and the electric hammer in the following projects. A solenoid device, too, has an iron core and a coil of wire. But in a solenoid device, the core is always outside the coil. For the solenoid itself is the coil of wire carrying the current. When the electrical current passes through the coil, the iron core is sucked in.

The solenoid also has many practical uses. It is used in many electrical devices wherever an electrical impulse must be changed into a pushing or pulling action. For instance, a solenoid forms the heart of many kinds of relays, contactors, and circuit breakers. One such example is found in the automatic washing machine. Here the solenoid makes the different changes in the washing process possible.

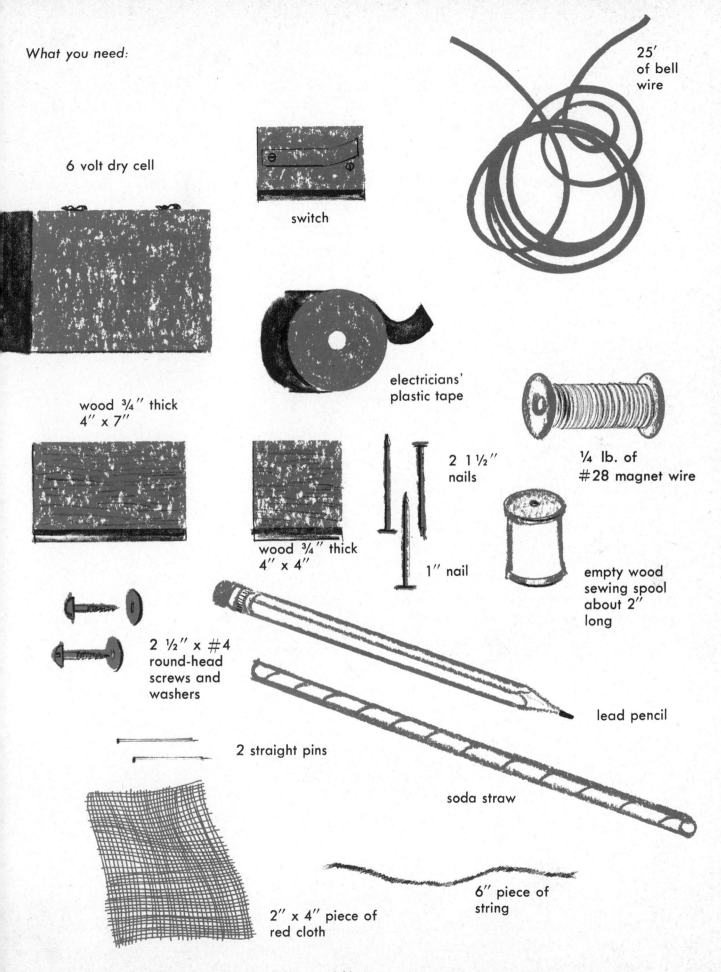

What you need:

6 volt dry cell

switch

25' of bell wire

electricians' plastic tape

wood ¾" thick 4" x 7"

wood ¾" thick 4" x 4"

2 1½" nails

1" nail

¼ lb. of #28 magnet wire

empty wood sewing spool about 2" long

2 ½" x #4 round-head screws and washers

lead pencil

2 straight pins

soda straw

2" x 4" piece of red cloth

6" piece of string

141

Using the two 1 ½″ nails, fasten one end of the larger wood blocks across the middle of the smaller one. This makes the flag mounting stand.

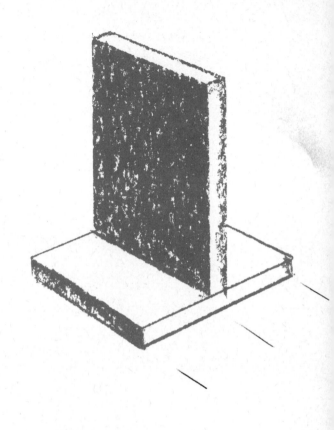

Drill a hole about 1″ from the top and ½″ from the edge of the mounting stand as shown. The hole should be just large enough for the lead pencil to fit tight. A 5/16″ hole is about right for most pencils.

Wind about 300 layers of #28 magnet wire around the spool. Leave about 8″ sticking out at each end. Be sure to wind the turns of wire tight and as close to each other as possible. Also be sure to remove all kinks before winding the wire in place.

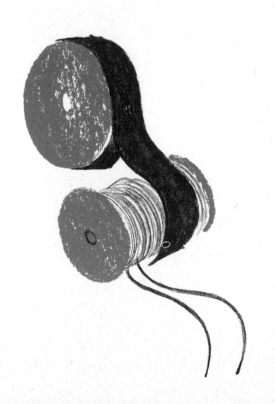

Keep the wire from unwinding by wrapping a couple of turns of electricians' tape around the coil.

Push the pencil through the hole almost up to the eraser.

Using plastic electricians' tape or Scotch tape, fasten the spool of magnet wire 1″ from the edge and about 1½″ from the bottom of the wood upright piece.

With a pair of scissors, cut the piece of cloth into a three cornered flag.

Fasten the flag with Scotch tape or glue to the end of the soda straw.

Push a straight pin through the soda straw into the eraser about 3¼″ from the end opposite the flag. Work the soda straw up and down until the pin fits loosely.

Using the piece of string, tie the 1″ nail near the end of the soda straw so that its point hangs just inside of the hole in the spool. You may find it necessary later on to readjust the pencil's position slightly.

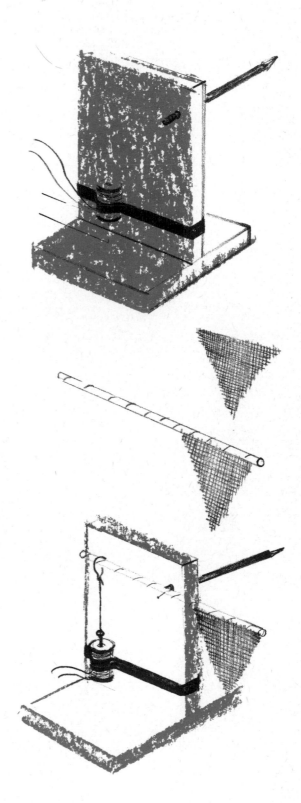

Keep the straw level by pushing the second pin in the wood upright just above the straw.

Fasten the two round-head screws and washers to the baseboard of the mounting stand. These serve as terminals.

Using a short piece of bell wire, connect the battery to the switch.

Scrape the insulation from the wires sticking out of the coil. Then connect each one to a round-head terminal screw on the baseboard. Also, using bell wire, connect the remaining terminals on the battery and switch to the terminals on the baseboard.

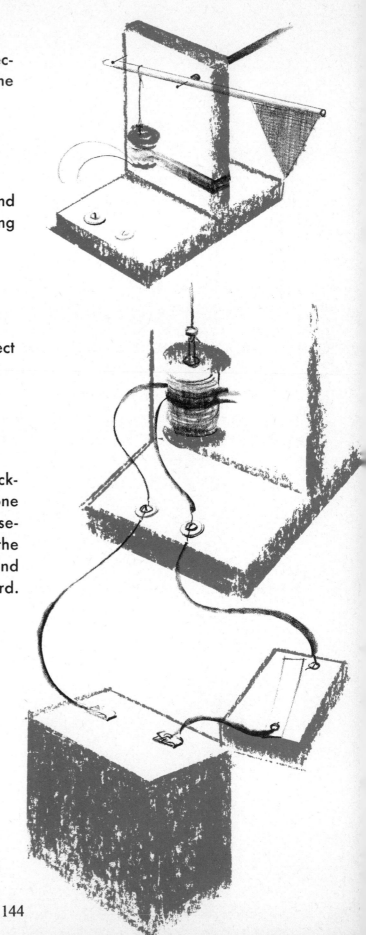

Quickly close and open the switch several times. If everything is in good working order, the nail moves in and out of the coil, causing the flag to wave up and down. If it doesn't wave up and down, some adjustments may be in order. Try changing the distance between the flag end of the straw and the eraser. Simply push the pin through the straw at different points until you find the spot where the flag works best. Also be sure the nail point always hangs just inside the center of the hole in the spool.

Also a few wads of chewing gum placed on one end of the soda straw may give the balance needed for the flag to work at its best.

The electric hammer is a fascinating and interesting project. It is fascinating to watch the machine bolt, which is the hammer, rise and fall. Of course you will know this coil to be a solenoid. And you expect this sort of thing to happen. But most of your friends will wonder and wonder some more as you give a demonstration.

Electric hammer

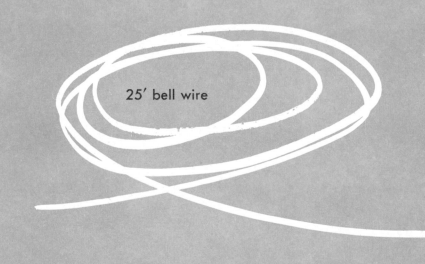

25' bell wire

thumb tack

switch

⅜″ (outside diameter) x
4¾″ copper tubing
(Glass or paper tubing can be used.)

It is an interesting project because you will actually make a model electric hammer. With it you can give demonstrations to your friends. In your demonstrations, you will be able to break toothpicks, drive thumb tacks in soft wood, and do many other little tasks that will amaze your friends.

What you need:

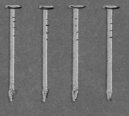

4 #6 box nails

bracket pieces

board ¾″ thick
6″ x 6″

¾″ x 2″ x 2¾″

¾″ x 2″ x 4½″

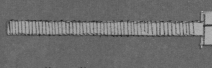

¼″ x 4″ machine bolt

piece of cork
cut from a
bottle cork

6 volt dry cell

Using a 5/32" wood bit, drill a hole in the ¾" x 2" x 2¾" wood bracket piece as shown.

Fasten the two wood bracket pieces together with two #6 box nails.

Beginning three-fourths of an inch from one end of the copper tube, wind about 100 turns of bell wire in the same direction. (One hundred turns requires winding the wire to the opposite end of the tube and back to the starting point.) Be sure to leave about a foot of wire at each end. Keep the wire coil tight by twisting the two end wires together.

Next force the bare end of the copper pipe through the bracket hole. CAUTION: If the hole is too small, ream it out with a piece of sandpaper or a small, sharp knife blade.

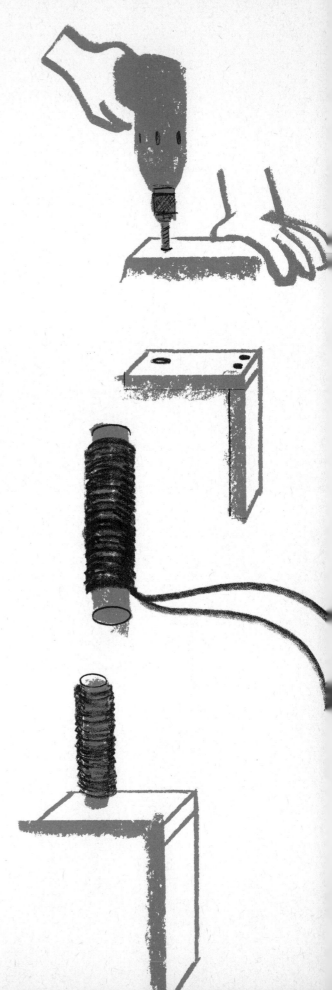

Now place the ¼″ machine bolt (head down) in the copper tube. Then using two box-6 nails, complete the bracket by nailing the assembled part to the baseboard.

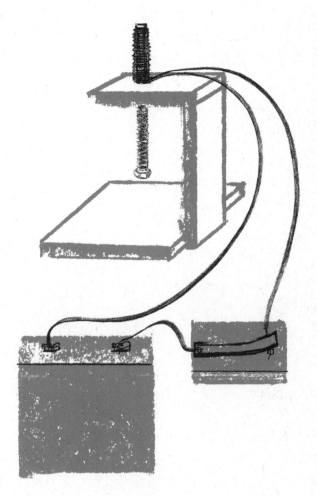

Scrape about an inch of insulation from the ends of the two coil wires. Connect one wire to a battery terminal. CAUTION: Never connect the solenoid coil wires directly to a 110-120 volt circuit.

Connect the second coil wire to one of the switch terminals. Using a short piece of bell wire, connect the second switch terminal to the remaining battery terminal.

You just made an electric hammer. When you press the switch, a magnetic current is made, causing the bolt to be sucked up into the coil. Releasing the switch causes the bolt to drop with a thud. Of course gravity is the force that causes the bolt to drop. When you release the switch, you open the circuit.

You can show your friends how the electric hammer works. Place the point of a thumb tack in a thin piece of cork or soft wood. Press the switch. Place the cork and thumb tack directly underneath the bolt. Release the switch. Pressing and releasing the switch several times causes the bolt to rise and fall. These operations drive the thumb tack into the cork. Your electric hammer can also break tooth picks propped against a pencil.

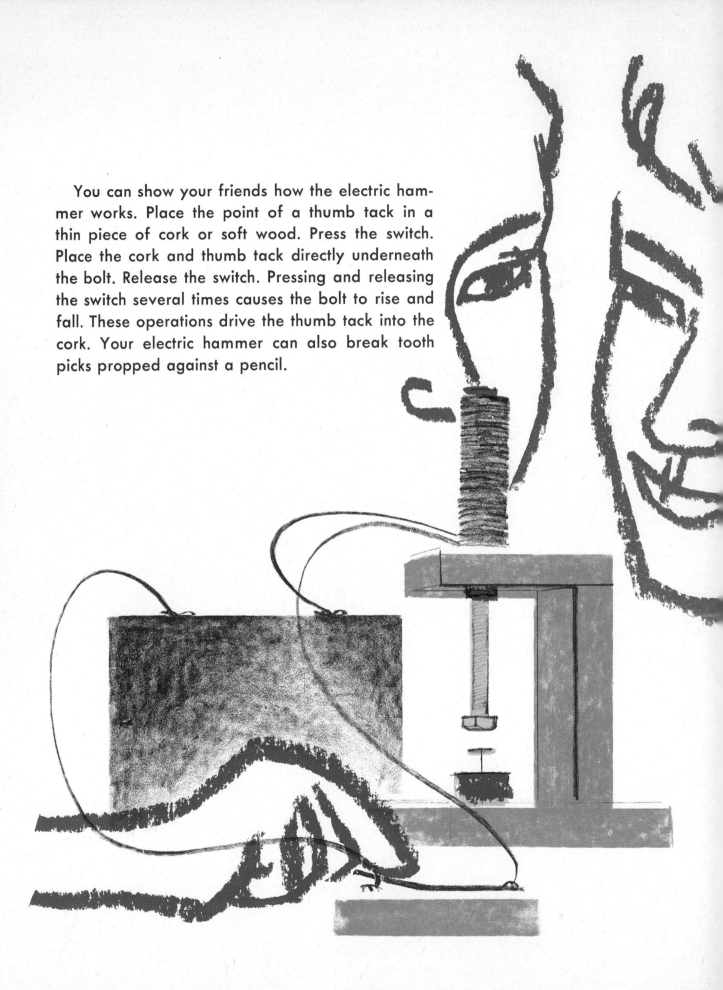

Keys to better projects give you important tips on working more easily with electrical projects. As you work with electricity, you will find these tips are worth keeping in mind.

Twelve keys to better projects

1. Most electric devices generate heat. As long as they do not overheat, there is no danger. So it is a good idea to touch any electric device with caution, especially after it has just been used. Remember, even some light bulbs generate enough heat to cause severe burns.

2. Sometimes a current flows through an easy short cut instead of going through the regular circuit. This is called a *short circuit*. It is a good idea not to short circuit dry cells for more than a few seconds at any one time, if you must. To do so shortens their lives.

3. Always hold the plug when inserting it or pulling it out of an electric outlet. To put pressure on the cord itself, is to invite trouble. If the wires are pulled apart, a bad short circuit can develop.

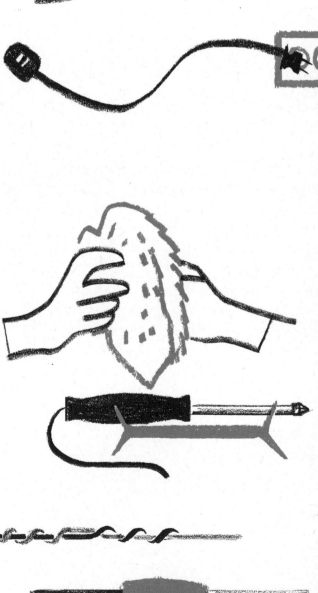

4. Electric cords or wiring should be well insulated at all times. Never take a chance, like running an extension cord under a rug. If the insulation wears off, a short circuit might occur that could cause a fire.

5. Hands and feet should be perfectly dry when working with any electric device. Water is a good conductor of electricity. So water on the body in contact with a short circuit can cause death. This is even true with ordinary house current of only 110 volts.

6. While working with electric projects, you will be lucky if you don't need to make several splices because of broken wires. There are usually three ways to do this:
   a. Wrap the wires around each other.
   b. Wrap the wires around each other, soldering them together. Soldering instructions are given in key number 12.

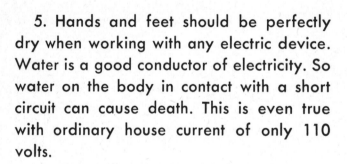

c. Wrap the wires between the head of a bolt and washer, tightening the nut makes for a good connection.

(Always wrap a wire or wires clockwise when making a connection where a bolt or screw is used. To do otherwise causes the end of the wire to work away from the bolt or screw rather than work toward it.)

7. When making connections, generally leave a little more wire than needed. This can be wrapped around a pencil, forming a pig tail. Then if the wire breaks, there is always plenty left without having to make a splice.

8. In the first project, you learn how to make a light bulb socket. With it, a bulb, a few feet of bell wire, a dry cell, and a switch, you have an excellent check light. It can be used to see if dry cells and flashlight batteries are good. You can use it to check circuits in your projects to see if they are open or closed. Notice how it is used in the picture to check the coil. If the light bulb burns, the coil is good. If the light bulb does not burn, it means there is a break somewhere in one of the coils of wire.

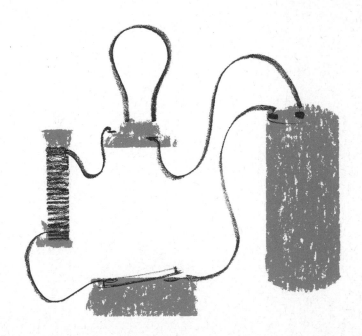

9. Whenever you want to use two or more dry cells for a project, use a 6 volt electric lantern battery instead.

One can be found in any hardware store for the cost of about three 1 ½ volt dry cells.

10. If you need pulleys for some of your electric projects, you can make them easily from empty sewing spools.

With a fine-tooth saw, cut away a section of a sewing spool so that about ⅛″ of the spool remains with each flange.

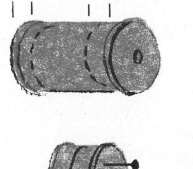

Using 3 small brads, fasten the spool back together. You now have a pulley for about a ¼″ shaft, which is large enough for a heavy string belt.

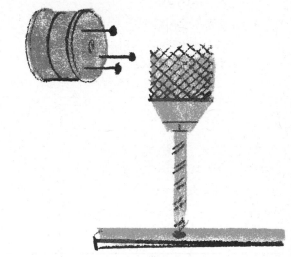

Prepare the shaft for mounting the pulley in one of two ways:

1. Drill a ⅛″ hole through the axle in the center of the pulley location or

2. File a ⅛″ V in the axle in the center of the pulley location.

Slide the pulley into position. Drive a small nail through the pulley shaft and hole in axle. This keeps the pulley from slipping.

If the hole in the pulley is larger than the axle, take up the play with four small, wood wedges of equal size. Match sticks trimmed to size work well. Four wedges instead of one large one make the pulley run on center. This causes the pulley to run true.

11. Many of the projects make use of an electromagnet of one kind or another. Perhaps you would like to make some magnets stronger in some cases. If so, here are two ways to do it:

   a. Increase the number of coils in the electromagnet.
   b. Increase the voltage in the coil. If you are using a certain number of dry cells, add more to the circuit.

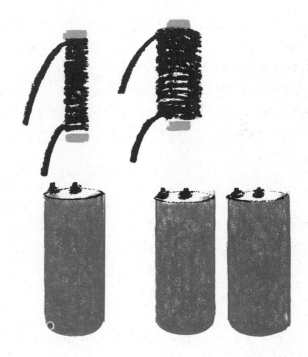

12. You can not work long with electricity without wishing you could solder. If you do exactly as directed, you can soon become an expert with a soldering iron.

If you have a small common soldering iron that is heated in a gas flame, use it. If you must buy one, get an electric iron from a hardware store. In either case, the directions are the same except for heating and reheating the iron.

A 75-watt electric soldering iron will do the job for ordinary soldering needed for projects in this book or for radios. If you intend to solder large pieces of sheet metal, an iron of at least 150 watts is needed.

Here are seven easy steps to follow for successful soldering.

Using sandpaper or steel wool, thoroughly clean the parts to be soldered. The parts of copper wires to be soldered must also be free of insulation. Enamel coating covering some wires must be completely removed.

Apply soldering flux to the parts to be soldered. The purpose of a flux is to prevent oxidation of the metal by the air.

Flux may be secured from any hardware store. Copper, brass or any non-ferrous metals call for non-corrosive soldering paste. Galvanized steel and other ferrous metals call for 15 per cent zinc chloride solution as a flux.

Next prepare the soldering iron by tinning it. Begin by filing all four sides of the tip of the iron. It must be free of nicks and cuts. The point must be about 1/8″ square.

Heat the iron until a steady green flame is coming off for a minute or two. Now put a small piece of solder into powdered sal ammoniac or put it on a sal ammoniac block. (Sal ammoniac may be bought in any hardware store.) Rub the tip of the heated iron over the sal ammoniac. For a good tinning job, the tip of the iron should be coated with solder, wiping excess away with steel wool.

Tin the parts to be soldered. Using the point of the heated iron, add solder to the already prepared fluxed surface.

Now place the two surfaces together and apply the heated iron up and down the joint. The two surfaces will join together when the metal is hot enough to melt the solder between them. Allow joint to cool before testing.

For soldering copper wire joints, place the fluxed joint, as shown in key 6, picture #2, on heated iron. Apply the solder directly to the wires. Soon they will be hot enough to melt the solder, forming a nice metal-coated joint. Always use electricians' tape to insulate such joints.

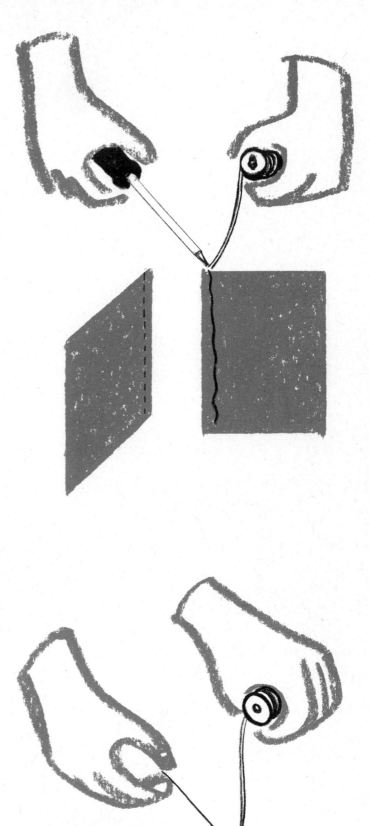

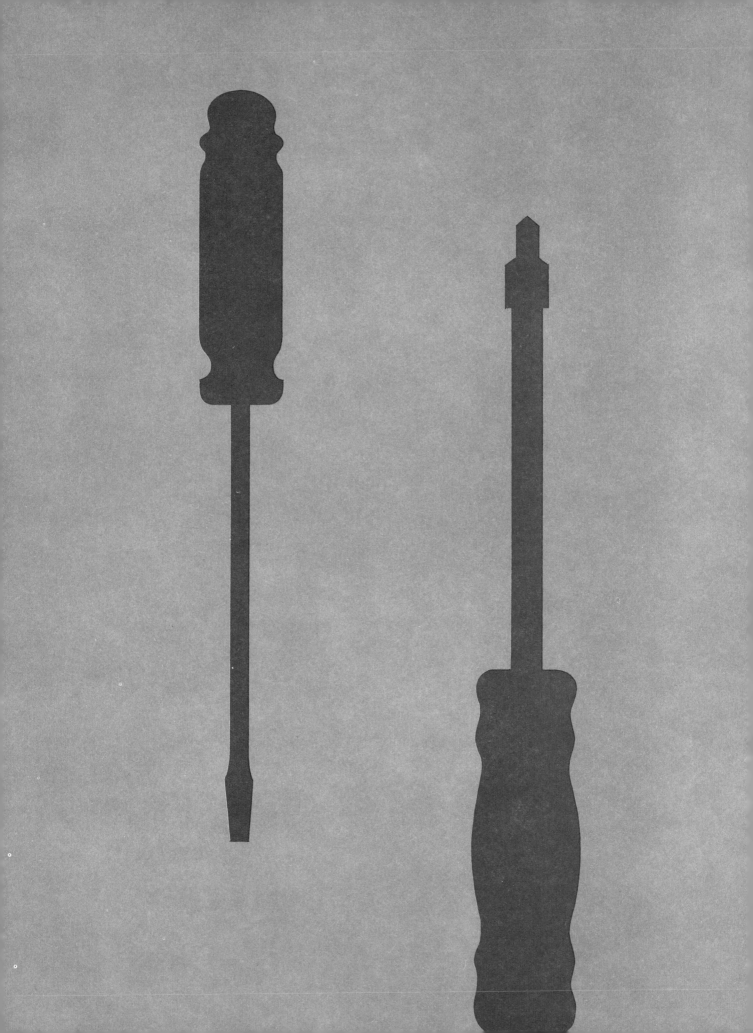

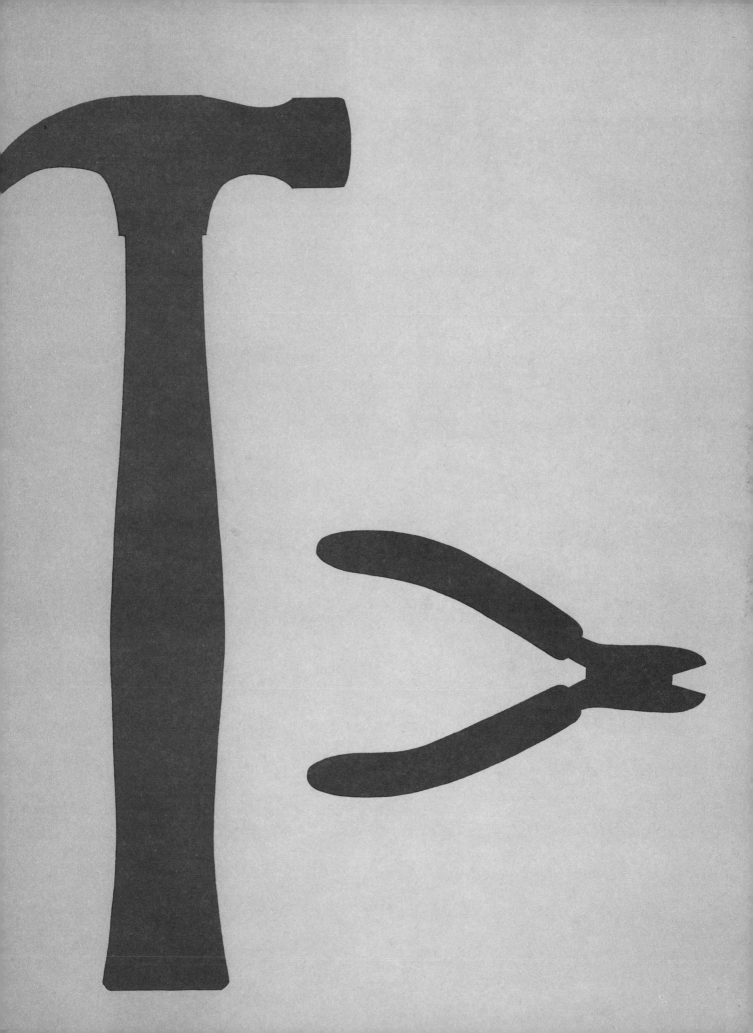